"Let Tracey Gendron take you on a unique, profound, well-written, and well-explained exploration of ageism. Personal experiences of her own family history — similar to those that many of us have experienced — serve to connect Gendron's years of study and research on ageism. As the title suggests, Gendron 'unmasks' what ageism really is, in practice, in society, in the workplace, in our daily lives. Ageism is finally making the headlines and becoming a subject of global attention thanks to researchers like Gendron who for decades have been trying to translate knowledge from their field for a broad audience without over-simplifying or trivializing ideas and information that for too long has remained in university lecture halls and gerontology conferences. Not reading this book would perhaps be your biggest mistake of the year."

> — Prof. Nic Palmarini, Director of the National
> Innovation Centre for Ageing

"Books that combine the rigor of a scholar with the passion of an advocate are rare and invaluable. *Ageism Unmasked* is one of them. With wit and skill, Tracey Gendron describes the ongoing, multi-faceted nature of human aging; deconstructs the historical and social forces that frame it as decline; and asks us to think boldly and imaginatively about the years ahead. *Ageism Unmasked* is essential reading for everyone who aspires to purpose and meaning right to the end and is willing to challenge the ageism and ableism that stand in our way."

> — Ashton Applewhite, author of *This Chair Rocks:*
> *A Manifesto Against Ageism*

"This book is a must-read for anyone who is aging — and that is every one of us! *Ageism Unmasked* takes the reader on a journey of understanding the roots of ageism, its impact, and what each of us can do to create a new reality of elderhood. It's a fascinating and inspirational read — a true game-changer and society-changer!"

> — Jill Vitale-Aussem, author of *Disrupting*
> *the Status Quo of Senior Living*

"This book manages the near impossible feat of being simultaneously broad, deep, and impactful. These pages treat readers to a fascinating exploration of where ageism comes from and what we can do to unmask (and undo) its pernicious workings. If *Ageism Unmasked* is as widely read and studied as it deserves to be, we will all be better off for it."

— Dr. Bill Thomas, author of *Aging Magnificently*

"*Ageism Unmasked* challenged me to think in new ways about unconscious age bias and the insidious way it shows up (even when unwelcomed) in everyday attitudes and actions. A must-read for policymakers, advertisers, health care workers and aging services professionals, and anyone grappling with their own age-related issues or those of an older relative or friend, *Ageism Unmasked* offers insight and guidance on concrete actions individuals and organizations alike can take in their fight against age bias and discrimination."

— Elizabeth White, author of *55,
Underemployed and Faking Normal*

"Tracey Gendron has written a fascinating exploration of the one '-ism' that impacts all of us, at every point in our lives. This book will challenge everything you thought you knew about ageism and how it affects you personally, no matter who or how old you are, and shows how all of us can play a part in overturning this ridiculous barrier to doing better business and living happier lives."

— Cindy Gallop, Founder & CEO of MakeLoveNotPorn

AGEISM UNMASKED

Exploring Age Bias and How to End It

Tracey Gendron, PhD

STEERFORTH PRESS
LEBANON, NEW HAMPSHIRE

For information about permission to reproduce
selections from this book, write to:
Steerforth Press L.L.C., 31 Hanover Street, Suite 1
Lebanon, New Hampshire 03766

Cataloging-in-Publication Data is available from the Library of Congress

Printed in the United States of America

ISBN 978-1-58642-322-3

1 3 5 7 9 10 8 6 4 2

To Nonny and Poppy.
Forever my role models and source of inspiritation.

Contents

Preface

Everything you know about aging is wrong. It's not your fault. Everything you have been taught about aging is wrong. From a young age, our developing brains are flooded with images, songs, and stories that stoke fears of being old. Our beloved bedtime stories are filled with older characters portrayed as ugly, scary, silly, or feeble. As we grow up, we hear our parents speak disparagingly about feeling old and watch as they make concerted efforts to act young to stay relevant. In elementary school, we blindly participate in activities like the widespread practice of celebrating the one hundredth day of school with a "dress like a one-hundred-year-old day" activity that creates caricatures of old people. As teens, we are utterly unaware that our favorite songs teem with ageist lyrics. In early adulthood, we are the primary targets of marketing for anti-aging cosmetics and products and are told that it is never too soon to fight aging.

Messages suggesting that healthy aging means being active, independent, and physically and cognitively robust wash over us. We equate any amount of dependence as failure. Our expectations are unrealistic. As mortal beings, we eventually and inevitably experience physical decline. The truth is that we are never independent but always interdependent. Cultural messaging presents caregiving as a burden that leads to burnout rather than a natural and normal part of human relationships. The beauty and reciprocity inherent in providing and receiving care get lost.

Even the most well-intentioned efforts to educate people about aging are often misleading and damaging. Old-age simulation suits that mimic aspects of aging have been created to help build empathy for old people. As if a suit can give us any meaningful insight into what it is like to be any given older person. As if older people are a monolithic group where everyone ages in a predictable pattern.

Attempts to be anti-ageist fall into perilous traps that fuel, rather than dismantle, ageism. We throw around terms like *ageless, feel young, you're only as old as you feel,* and *never get old* as anti-ageist strategies. We fail to see that these sentiments are themselves ageist. Using the term *ageless* denies age. It screams out, "I don't see age." But we need to see age. It is a vital part of our human identity, and of the human condition. Hard-earned life lessons and experience enable us to become fully realized. They should be not just recognized, but venerated. Using strategies that downplay or ignore the aging process to fight ageism is like putting out a fire with an extinguisher filled with kerosene.

This book will help you recognize how ageism and ableism are endemic in our culture, and how they have become ingrained in your thinking. Understanding the history of ageism will help you to develop the knowledge, skills, and strategies necessary to disrupt ageism and ableism within yourself and to help others do the same. We can't do better until we know better. It's time for us to grow up, let go of our desperate need to stay young, and embrace that we age and get old.

Introduction

Not so long ago, I realized that I was repeatedly being asked the same question: "Are you okay?" My kids, husband, friends, coworkers, and, once or twice, new acquaintances were asking me this, almost always with a slightly bemused expression.

Had there been a camera trained on me just before the question got asked, it would have captured me gesticulating wildly and grumbling — perhaps even hurling questions and insults — at a TV screen, or maybe the car radio or a magazine I'd just thrown back down.

What was getting me so worked up? *Ageism.* The shame-inducing, anxiety-producing, guilt-mongering force in our culture that is both everywhere and all but invisible. Advertisements and media tell us what to look like, how to feel, and what to value. Even those who are attuned to this might feel like they can avoid falling prey, but practically and psychologically we are all susceptible to all-pervasive meta-narratives. You might know that the latest look-younger product is nothing more than snake oil, but your brain still does the equations: younger = good; older = bad.

We live in a culture of manipulation. We can't escape it, but we can learn to recognize it, and perhaps begin to change it. I was a senior in high school when I took my first psychology class and discovered that the size of the aging population was growing rapidly. A new term entered my lexicon: *gerontology.* I learned that gerontology is the scientific study of aging from biological, psycho-logical, social, and spiritual perspectives within a holistic framework that focuses on the individual within the context of their environment. Gerontologists take a person-centered approach that prioritizes individuals' needs, preferences, and values to personalize and guide all aspects of aging and longevity. Gerontology is very different from geriatrics, a branch of medicine that focuses on older people's physical health and care. I found a discipline that was person-focused rather than problem-focused to be inspiring and set off on an academic journey that led to an undergraduate certificate in gerontology, a master's of science in gerontology, and a PhD in developmental psychology.

After about two decades in the field, I had an epiphany. I noticed that when others inquired about my career, I'd begin by explaining that I had a passion for working with the aging population. Why did I feel compelled to use the descriptor *aging* to refer to older adults and later life? I was a highly trained, experienced gerontologist and yet was referring to aging as something that happened to other people. *Those* people. *Old* people. I saw with real clarity for the first time that even I, someone who had dedicated her career to working with older people, had internalized an attitude toward aging as something undesirable, and I wanted to disassociate myself from looking, acting, or being old.

The meaning we assign to being old, and the concept of age identity, is socially constructed. Money is a social construct, too. Money, in and of itself, only has value because we assign it value; the paper that it is printed on has little objective worth. We create social constructs to help us make sense of the world, and they have a powerful influence on how we view people and how we interpret their behavior. Our understanding of what it means to *be old* exists because people have accepted it, not because it exists in objective reality.

With respect to age identity, we have an accepted understanding that old and young are two distinct and separate states of being. According to our social construct, young people embody stereotypical negative and positive attributes. They are prone to act irresponsibly, even dangerously, but they are also attractive, vibrant, and looking forward to promising futures.

Old people on the other hand, according to our social construct, are a homogeneous group comprising people who are frail, dependent, problematic, and fast on their way to becoming incompetent or irrelevant. Terms to describe individuals or groups of people in older age such as *aged, elderly, seniors, senior citizens*, and *old people* have been imbued with negative connotations. *Old*, in and of itself, can be an insulting pejorative.

We use the common understandings of old and young as a road map for the age-related behaviors we expect people to conform to. We expect young people to do stupid things like taking uncalculated risks, and we believe that old people will be content quietly sitting on a rocking chair watching the world go by. These assumptions will hold true for some people but will be way off base for others. Moreover, there is nothing about the actual definitions of *old* and *young* that should point to value judgments or behavioral expectations. The definition of *old* has to do with having lived or existed for a long time. The definition of *young* has to do with having lived or existed for a short time. Despite what you and I have been taught, young and old age are not either good or bad states of being — they just *are*.

I began to question my entire framework for understanding aging. I recognized that I had not yet disentangled what I learned about aging through my academic studies from what I knew about aging from the dominant cultural narrative. The dominant cultural narrative represents the sum total of stories and messages that we receive from the media, cultural institutions, social networks, and relationships. These messages shape our understanding of the world and influence our self-conceptions in insidious ways. Relational ageism, a concept developed by my colleagues Jenny Inker, Ayn Welleford, and me, describes how the norms represented in the dominant cultural narrative become internalized and are then perpetuated and reinforced in a social context.[1]

Relational ageism demonstrates how an ageist thought, belief, or attitude can spread from person to person through expression and support. For example, although the following interaction might seem innocuous, it powerfully shapes the dominant narrative about aging and being old:

> **John:** "Mary! So good to see you. You haven't aged a day since I saw you ten years ago!"
>
> **Mary:** "Thank you, John! What a nice thing to say. You just made my day."

This exchange may seem innocent on the surface, but looking more deeply, we see the value of *not looking or acting as if one has aged* being promoted and then *accepted through gratitude and thanks*. This is how relational ageism spreads from person to person like a silent contagion. Interactions like these occur on a daily basis, and the imbued meaning goes unchallenged. By disconnecting myself from the experience of aging, I had internalized and accepted these ideals. I used *aging* to reference older people when I proudly proclaimed that I dedicated my career to serve the growing aging population. I am not alone; this is a common occurrence. I give myself a pass for not knowing any better; you can't change what you don't see. After this realization, I set out to reconcile my belief system, starting with (re)defining what the term *aging* really means.

Aging is not something that just happens to older people. We all age, every moment of our lives, from birth through death. We routinely misuse the word *aging* in two ways. First, we use it to refer exclusively to older people rather than universally. This is true within my own discipline, where we describe people and organizations working with older adults as the aging services sector or aging-related industry. If we were to put aging into the perspective of a universal experience, we should then refer to preschools as part of the aging services sector, too. What a switch in perspective that would be! And doing so would be a step toward eliminating the disconnect between us (young) and them (old).

The term that accurately describes the process of biological aging is *senescence*:

- Senescence is the process of biological aging that leads to the gradual deterioration of function in cells and/or organisms.
- Aging, on the other hand, is the universal lifelong biological, psychological, social, and spiritual process of developing over time. Aging is dynamic and includes *all* processes, including growth, loss, maintenance, and adaptation. Aging is multidimensional and multidirectional.

Viewing the holistic and complex process of aging solely through the lens of biological senescence promotes a one-sided, decline-based view of aging. Using this framework, of course, we see aging as a process of slowly walking down a perilous slope until we inevitably fall off the cliff.

That is not the case!

Aging is a slow and steady process of *change* that ultimately leads to us becoming our unique, individual selves. Some of the ways we change are obvious, like growing taller or needing to use reading glasses, but other changes are much more subtle and harder to recognize. For example, as we age, we can regulate our emotions better. We've all seen a two-year-old have a temper tantrum when they don't get exactly what they want at the moment that they want it. But have you ever witnessed a grown-up drop to the floor kicking their feet and pounding their fists? You may have, but not likely. We don't need temper tantrums when we are older because we have learned valuable communication skills and have the advanced capacity to regulate emotions. Our lived experiences culminate to reduce the intensity of negative emotions and focus on feelings that promote happiness and calmness. This is aging. We have the correct terminology to distinguish between aging as growth and senescence as decline — so let's use it.

The epiphany that I was not self-identifying as an aging person subsequently provoked a new question: How had I failed to see the extent to which I held unexamined and unchallenged negative attitudes about aging? I spent the next few years digging deeper into research about ageism while concurrently reflecting upon and exploring my own attitudes about my own aging.

Attitudes represent emotional and mental states that influence thought and action. Attitudes about aging form the basis of ageism. Attitudes encompass our preferences and evaluations of people, objects, issues, and events, and they have three parts that intersect to influence how we think, feel, and act:

- **The cognitive component** of attitudes represents the beliefs and thoughts that form an opinion, or what we think. With ageism, cognitive attitudes come to light as stereotypes or generalities like "older people are bad drivers," or "all older people are frail."
- **The affective component** of attitudes is the emotional part of an attitude or what we feel. With respect to ageism, affective attitudes express prejudice, such as "I dislike being in the car with an older driver," or "I am uneasy around older people because they are frail."
- **The behavioral component** of attitudes consists of how we behave toward others and can lead to intentional and unintentional discrimination: "I will take the car keys away from someone that is old," or "I will not work with older people because they are frail."

Attitudes form the basis of our behaviors and can place us on the slippery slope to discrimination. We don't simply wake up one day and decide to be ageist. Instead, we are guided by a causal chain of events that influence our perceptions and behaviors:

- **A stereotype** is a distorted and simplified belief that attributes characteristics to members of a specific group. When we stereotype, we lump people together, thereby not acknowledging individual differences between group members.
- **Prejudice** is a judgment or unfavorable opinion or feeling formed without sufficient knowledge, thought, or reason. Prejudices can be learned as a result of stereotyping. Stereotypes and prejudices are problematic because they create discrimination.
- **Discrimination** is unjustified behavior toward different groups of people based on identity characteristics. Discriminatory behavior can lead to exclusion, oppression, marginalization, or even violence.

Let's use a workplace assignment scenario to illustrate how unintentional ageism can result from the cycle of discrimination: A sales manager is trying to secure a lucrative contract with a technology firm and needs to choose a project manager to represent their company in a sales pitch meeting. Two top performers are under consideration; one is in their sixties and one is in their twenties. For argument's sake, let's assume that the two candidates are comparable other than age. In considering the older candidate for the role, the hiring manager is experiencing a running commentary in their head that goes something like this:

I know that older people are not great with technology [stereotype], so given their age, I have some pretty significant reservations about their ability to lead this project [prejudice]. Based on that, I will pass the opportunity along to the other candidate [discrimination].

Let's flip this around and see how the ageist cycle of discrimination plays out in reverse:

> I know that younger people are lazy and want every-
> thing done their own way [stereotype], so given their
> age, I have some pretty significant reservations about
> their ability to lead this project [prejudice]. Based on
> that, I will pass the opportunity along to the other candi-
> date [discrimination].

In this case, the sales manager is wielding institutional power and has the official authority and capacity to decide the course of action to be taken. Their decision-making process will likely never be known to either candidate, and neither will know that they have been victims of discrimination, oppression, and marginalization. Oppression results from the combination of prejudice and institutional power, which creates a system that discriminates against certain groups (target group) and benefits other groups (dominant group). The oppressive power system limits the opportunities, rights, and freedoms of the target group. Marginalization results from using influence or power to place others in a position of lesser importance. Those in the dominant group experience privilege, which represents the rights, advantages, and benefits afforded to people at the expense of members of target groups.

Ageism results from discrimination, marginalization, and/or oppression based on age. Ageism against older people is widely prevalent, accepted, and based on a systemic value that idealizes youth over old age. Generally speaking, younger people are considered as the dominant group or in-group and older people are the target group or out-group. Ageism is a tremendously complex phenomenon that manifests in our health and well-being, in our relationships, policies, practices, and overall culture.

As we age, our physical bodies experience natural and normal physiological changes that decrease ability, stamina, and reserve capacity, making it impossible to fully disentangle ageism and ableism. Ableism is discrimination, marginalization, and/or oppression based on physical, intellectual, and/or cognitive ability.

Not all older people have disabilities and not all people with disabilities are older, but they both encounter discrimination and face stigma. People of advanced age who are cognitively challenged are even further stigmatized. The intersecting elements of naturally occurring physical decline of function in older age inextricably link and conceptually weave together ableism with ageism.

Fear of dependency is a side effect of ageism and ableism and is perpetuated by a widely held illusion of independence. Western culture is deeply immersed in the mentality of rugged individualism — "pull yourself up by your bootstraps" — and we have a misguided notion that maintaining independence and avoiding reliance on others is not only preferable but also admirable and expected. The truth is that we are never wholly independent, nor should we strive to be, especially as we grow older. Striving for complete independence sets the stage for dependence to be perceived as failure, further stigmatizing loss of ability and reinforcing the notion that caring for others is a "burden."

My realization that ageism and ableism are deeply embedded, normalized, invisible, and thriving within each of us hit me hard, made me sad and then angry — very angry. It was a catalyst to work on myself and to help guide others. Understanding ageism is not something that happens overnight. It is not as simple as an "ah-ha" moment, but not because the concept is difficult to grasp. It is not challenging to recognize that ageism is discrimination based on age. Ageism is hard to "get" because it's ubiquitous and we don't have a solid framework for an anti-ageism alternative. The truth is that the roots of ageism can be found throughout centuries of history. It's a complicated, insidious, imperceptible discrimination that has seeped into our everyday life and normalized the idea that it's scary and awful to be *old*. Most of the time this storyline is by cynical design, intended to elicit feelings of fear, shame, and guilt in an effort to inspire people to buy the necessary products and services required to age successfully or gracefully — or, more likely, to deny that we are aging at all.

Although ageism is commonly expressed as discrimination toward older people, it is inclusive of prejudice and oppression toward younger people. Everyday examples of youth-directed ageism can be found in comments that categorize, label, and generalize younger people as irresponsible, immature, or lazy. I prefer to use the term *ageism* to refer to all instances of discrimination based on age; however, *adultism* refers explicitly to discrimination, marginalization, and / or oppression against younger people based on age. Adultism is connected to generational bias (also called generational tension and generational conflict), which describes the belief that people in a particular generational group are inferior to another generation. It is postulated that generations develop similar social and historical reference points and cultural experiences that contribute to misunderstanding and / or tension among different age cohorts — Baby Boomers, Millennials, Generation X, et cetera. I firmly believe that the concept of generational tension, along with the notion of generations, is utter nonsense. It is simply not feasible to surmise that a group of people with a twenty- or thirty-year span in age have the same cultural experiences that shape similar attitudes, values, and ideals. Worse is that the contrived concept of generations leads to concocted rhetoric claiming that people in varying generations are so different from one another that they can't get along. I propose that ageism is the real underlying cause of tension.

All forms of ageism can be destructive to self-esteem, relationships, and the development of our future possible selves. Nevertheless, this book's primary focus is to critically evaluate ageism toward older people. There are three reasons why I think this approach is necessary:

- First, ageism facing older people represents a social justice and civil rights issue.
- Second, we don't have a ready alternative to the narrative of older adulthood as a period of decline — which

feeds our fears of aging and ageist thoughts and behaviors about all stages of life.

- Third, and most important, ageism has severe and damaging consequences to our health and happiness throughout our entire lives. Let me say that again to hammer it home. Ageism has significant repercussions for all of us at all stages of our lives.

Attitudes about aging are manifested and expressed as thoughts and behaviors toward self and others through several different dimensions of ageism. These dimensions are complex, layered, and mutually reinforcing; they have a cyclical effect whereby attitudes in one arena reinforce attitudes and behaviors in other arenas. For example, if you have negative feelings toward older people in general, you are more likely to struggle with negative feelings toward your own aging.

Other-directed ageism is tricky because it presents in both negative and positive ways. Negative ageism is the more damaging manifestation of prejudice resulting in exclusion and hostility. Positive ageism, or benevolent ageism, is based on a view of older people as warm but incompetent and translates into a form of prejudice that is masked with respect or kindness.[2] Benevolent ageism can be patronizing or infantilizing; it can lead to over-accommodating behaviors that limit older people's opportunities. Benevolent or compassionate ageism happens when we assume people need protecting based on their age alone. Stereotypes of older people as fragile or lonely provoke sympathy and behavior that may, or may not, be welcome. Helping someone cross the street is a lovely gesture. Assuming someone needs your help to cross the street because they look old is not.

Self-directed ageism, or internalized ageism, is how we feel about ourselves as an aging person. This represents the fear and anxiety associated with thoughts about aging ("I fear getting old"); denial of aging ("I am not old/I am still young"); and disassociation from or shame around aging ("I won't say how old I am in a group of people").

Remember, we learn about aging as a process of decline and loss. See for yourself. Do a quick online search of the keyword *aging* and see what comes up. I just did this myself, and I found a collection of links and articles that address topics such as "treatment and prevention," "reversing aging," and "bracing for the falls of an aging nation." Delightfully optimistic and an accurate portrayal of the dynamic process of growth and decline? No, of course not. Now try that with the keyword *childhood*, or *adolescence*, or even *adulthood*. Very different results with far fewer catastrophic and pessimistic outcomes. This exercise provides a quick glimpse into the dominant cultural narrative about aging as a process of decline that should be feared. In fact, this exercise also illustrates the dominant cultural description about old people as a frightening burden for society. These messages are inherently acts of manipulation. On the one hand, we are being manipulated into shame-based purchasing of products to make us look and feel younger. On the other hand, we are being manipulated into participating in scapegoating and blaming older people for the problems and issues society faces. Ageism is a type of manipulation, and manipulation impacts our health.

Cultural ageism drives this manipulation. Cultural ageism is the everyday, invisible, profoundly ingrained and normalized negative messages about aging and old people embedded in movies, TV, songs, jokes, greeting cards, birthday cards, literature, and language. We wade through the muck of negative depictions of aging every single day, and these sticky little messages persist by infecting our unconscious thoughts. They are pernicious and found in the advertisement you see for anti-aging supplements, the billboard you pass while driving that directs you to hide your wrinkles, and the song on the radio that quietly demoralizes being old. It is the dominant cultural narrative that devalues and deprioritizes older people. We have all read the articles proclaiming an impending crisis from a destructive tsunami of older people, leading to economic ruin and an unsustainable economy. In reality, ageism — the real manipulation — is the public health crisis taking a physical, mental, and emotional toll on all of us.

To add another layer of complexity, we are often entirely unaware that these sticky little messages infiltrate our thoughts. Implicit ageism is the unconscious bias that includes attitudes, feelings, and behaviors toward people of other age groups that operates without conscious awareness or intention.[3] It's sneaky and hard to detect. It's something that gets automatically activated, which in turn makes it really dangerous. For example, imagine a situation in which you are waiting in the checkout line at a store and an older person is at the front of the line at the cashier. The older person begins to use their cell phone to access information, and your immediate reaction is a mounting sense of frustration because you assume an older person working a cell phone will take forever. Right there, at that moment, you have made an automatic negative assumption based solely on a person's age. This is implicit ageism. The negative consequences of ageism are severe and wide reaching, and the research provides ample evidence as to why this should matter to each and every one of us.

Why Should I Care?

I would bet that through your life, you have heard that smoking cigarettes, not getting enough sleep, not getting enough exercise, being lonely or socially isolated, and not using sunscreen are all things that are bad for your health. Information on these risk factors and many others like them has circulated freely for years. But did you know that there is also an abundance of research on ageism's physical, psychological, social, and economic consequences? The general population is largely unaware of the findings of more than two decades of evidence-based research into the effects of ageism.

Ageism Matters Because It Is Bad for Your Health

- People with positive attitudes toward aging live on average seven and a half years longer than those with negative attitudes.[4] Seriously, seven and a half years of your life is potentially wrapped up in how you feel about your own aging!
- The stress of ageism contributes to an increased risk of chronic disease.[5]
- Self-directed ageism is associated with a higher presence of markers of Alzheimer's disease.[6]
- Self-directed ageism is associated with lower physical and cognitive function.[7]
- Negative self-perceptions of aging are related to physical losses and depressive symptoms.[8]
- Negative self-perceptions of aging lead to poorer self-rated health and decreased autonomy.[9]
- Younger people who hold more negative age stereotypes have a greater likelihood of experiencing cardiovascular events in the following four decades than those with positive age stereotypes.[10]
- Older people with low expectations of aging well are more likely to believe it is not important to seek health care.[11]
- People with more negative aging attitudes have increased emotional reactions to daily stressors.[12]

Ageism Matters Because It Is Bad for Business

Data from a variety of sectors show that ageism impacts economic output, consumer spending, the workplace, and industry:

- Older people are kept out of production roles, hindering their ability to make money and to contribute to economic growth.[13]
- Because of ageism, industries systematically focus only on the safety and security needs of older adults, such as assistive devices, alert systems, and hearing aids, leav-

ing a scarcity of products and services that focus on growth, well-being, and self-actualization for the same population.[14]

- Ageism has created a dearth in marketing and advertising — only about 5 percent of US advertising is aimed at people over fifty. And yet people over fifty dominate spending across most categories.[15]
- Ageism has a price tag of $63 billion annually in health care costs. Ageism is responsible for 17.04 million cases of the eight most expensive health conditions per year among those sixty and older.[16]
- Ageism impacts job satisfaction and career commitment for those working with older adults. Essentially, ageism impacts job recruitment and retention, which has major economic implications.[17]
- Age-based workplace discrimination obstructs older Americans from fulfilling their potential and creates a strain on economic growth.[18]

Ageism Matters Because It Contributes to Inequity

Ageism strips away economic, political, and social rights and opportunities for older people. It's a civil rights issue because it creates barriers for older people to access political and social freedom and equality:

- Ageism leads to social exclusion of older people within their neighborhoods.[19]
- The quality, delivery, and amount of health care received is impacted by ageism.[20]
- One of every seventeen adults over fifty years of age experiences health care discrimination, which contributes to new or worsened disability.[21]
- The number of age-related discrimination charges filed with employers and the EEOC by workers aged sixty-five and older doubled from 1990 to 2017.[22]

I am susceptible to the effects of ageism, and so are you. The complex, multilayered, multidimensional nature of ageism requires that we critically evaluate our guiding assumptions about aging to unlearn and relearn in a more holistic, healthy, and productive way. I have spent the past fifteen years peeling away layer after layer to uncover my own hidden assumptions and biases about aging, only to discover there is so much more that I haven't unearthed and don't yet comprehend.

The process of discovery and self-realization necessary to disrupt the ageism festering within each of us will be unique and deeply personal. The way we experience aging, and therefore ageism, is contingent upon our other forms of identity. Kimberlé Crenshaw coined the term *intersectionality* to capture overlapping and independent systems of discrimination and privilege that intersect to influence life experiences and create multiple layers of marginalization. For example, the impact of ageism cannot be completely disentangled from experiences with other forms of discrimination such as racism, sexism, classism, sexual orientation, and gender identity. Aging, as well as ageism, does not exist in a vacuum, and every individual will experience it differently.

Ageism is incredibly complicated. Although it has commonalities with many other forms of discrimination, it is unique in many ways, including that it is something everyone will encounter and is essentially the manifestation of our prejudice toward our future selves.

But there is very good news: Once you begin to recognize ageism in all its forms, you will be able to make conscious choices on how you want to experience aging. You have the power and the ability to create your version of elderhood. We are all undoubtedly familiar with the common terminology for the stages of life. We commonly use terms like *infancy*, *toddlerhood*, *childhood*, *adolescence*, and *adulthood* to describe developmental stages. After adulthood we talk about being in the stage of older adulthood, our senior years, retirement, or old age. Fundamentally, none of those terms adequately portray growth and development in later life. The term *older adulthood* is problematic because it reinforces a narrow view of older age as the continuation of roles and interests of adulthood. *Senior years*, *retirement*, and *old age* are deficit-based terms that don't convey the developmental tasks and opportunities in later life.

Until recently, we haven't had a specific term for a developmental stage past adulthood. Writers and advocates Louise Aronson and Bill Thomas have embraced the word *elderhood* to describe the complex, multidirectional, multidimensional phenomenon that is the capstone of the aging experience. I define *elderhood* as a developmental stage of life that encompasses older age. Elderhood involves dynamic and simultaneous processes of decline, maintenance, adaptation, and intellectual, socio-emotional, psychological, and spiritual growth. I use the term *elder* to describe someone who is in the developmental stage of elderhood. After all, we refer to a child in childhood, an adolescent in adolescence, and an adult in adulthood.

If you have a visceral negative reaction to the term *elder* and find that you wouldn't want to be identified as such, I encourage you to think about why that may be. I suggest that it's because we have deeply stigmatized what it means to be old. Individually and collectively, we have the ability to reframe elderhood as a time in life with the potential for meaningful growth and development that accompanies an acceptance of physical decline and mortality. *Elderhood* is a term with power and purpose, and I believe it holds the key to an anti-ageist world.

This book takes a journey through time to reveal the forces that have shaped our understanding of aging and what it means to be old. The purpose of this journey is to reveal what has become largely invisible. We must recognize and understand the forces that have created the present to craft a purposeful path to a better future. This historical account will help us understand the factors that have contributed to our beliefs and misconceptions about aging and explain the deficiency in our current understanding and acknowledgment of elderhood.

By learning from the past, we will develop tools to empower ourselves and others to create an anti-ageist world built upon the foundation of elderhood. To be anti-ageist means that we develop the knowledge and skills to disrupt ageist and ableist thought and behavior within ourselves, communities, policy, and culture. We can learn how to create a path forward to a world based on age equity that acknowledges and embraces elderhood.

CHAPTER ONE

Complicated from the Beginning

Study the past if you would define the future.

— Confucius

I remember details about my paternal grandparents as if I saw them just last week. I can visualize every room of their three-bedroom house, the patio with lush greenery, and the artifacts from their travels placed all around their home with care. When I close my eyes, I can hear classical music playing and the sounds of the referee's whistle from Sunday football games on the television. I can still smell the chocolatey goodness of homemade brownies emanating from the kitchen. Nonny and Poppy had no idea that they were profoundly influencing my career path by simply living — *aging* — in my presence. Both of them were talented and accomplished people. Nonny was a Juilliard-trained concert pianist; Poppy was a medical doctor specializing in pulmonary disorders and assistant commissioner of hospitals in New York. As they aged, I watched them continue to grow and evolve. Nonny gave piano lessons; she entertained and baked, read books, and traveled internationally. Poppy did grand rounds once a week at the hospital, took up photography, and attended classes at a local university. He traveled internationally with my grandmother, but reluctantly, because of a sensitive stomach that had difficulty handling anything aside from peanut butter and jelly. Simultaneously, I saw them slow down physically. My cousin and I took over dish duty at Thanksgiving; it was clear it had become too challenging for them to manage.

They moved more deliberately and cautiously. Watching them, I witnessed firsthand the rich and complex stories of their aging: a story of growth, a story of loss, and a story of resilience.

Nonny and Poppy's son, my father, is now in his midseventies and has been married to my mom for fifty-four years. We are a close family, and my children have grown up seeing their grandparents many times a week, every week. I continue to learn by watching their aging unfold and listening to them when they impart their experiences, and I have the added benefit of sharing my insights as a gerontologist with them. The physical and emotional closeness we share allows for direct observation of how personal and nuanced aging is. I'm reminded of the fact that aging is a universal process and yet distinctive and unique to the individual. My parents each have their own fears, anxieties, goals, wants, and needs.

One of the most challenging aspects of doing my job as a gerontologist is that I have not personally experienced old age. I can infer from my knowledge of theory and evidence-based practice. I can empathize with the biological changes that occur and alter bodily functions. I can create opportunities that encourage emotional, spiritual, and psychological growth. But I can't *know*. As an educational gerontologist, I can use this concept of not knowing to my advantage when I teach others; no one can really know what it is like to walk in another's shoes. A common saying in my classroom is, "Once you have met one older person, you have met one older person." In other words, it is a mistake to suppose or generalize what it is like to age for any one person. Our path to aging is inextricably linked to all forms of our identity (race, gender, caste, class, sexuality, religion, disability, weight, height), which dictate how we experience the world and how the world responds to us. The overlapping layers of our identity mean that as we age, we become more unique and less alike as a group — a concept called the individuation of aging. Each person has their unique path and trajectory, which shape their understanding and experience of growing older.

Many of us are fortunate enough to have positive role models who shape our understanding of later life and our relationship with the aging process. Nonetheless, we are all exposed to the harmful and misleading cultural messages and narratives suggesting that later life is a declining slope of decrepitude. Even with the example of Nonny and Poppy informing my understanding of what aging could be, it has taken me decades of learning, reflecting, challenging biases, and relearning to appreciate (rather than fear) the beautiful complexities of the aging experience. I have found that the story of how older people are viewed, esteemed, and paradoxically devalued has evolved and taken many twists and turns throughout history and across cultures. Let's start from the beginning.

The History of Elders and Reverence

Some of the earliest historical references are found in religious and ancient texts. A brief overview illustrates that ancient cultures valued older people for their experience, knowledge, and survival skills. Although old age is rarely discussed in the Judeo-Christian Bible, long-lived people are regarded as favored by God to fulfill a divine purpose. Early references to the value of old age can be found in various expressions and Bible verses. For example, the Hebrew word *zagen*, which roughly translates as "well advanced in years," was applied to multiple noble functions and tasks. Leviticus 19:32 includes these words: "Rise in the presence of the aged, show respect for the elderly [*zagen*] and revere your God." The term *elder* has connotations indicating political responsibility and influence in referring to chief servants (2 Samuel 12:17), a group of older men entrusted with governmental affairs (Exodus 3:16), and "the elders of Israel" who accompanied Moses on his first meeting with the King of Egypt (Exodus 3:18) and at the ratification of the Sinai covenant (Exodus 17:5). There are also examples of respect or veneration shown to older people in New Testament passages that include

Paul addressing elders as "overseers" (Acts 20:17) and Peter calling them "shepherds" (1 Peter 5:1–2).

Elders became the official religious leadership in the early church and were appointed as overseers (sometimes called bishops) for local congregations (Acts 14:23). In 1 Timothy, the term *elder* is used interchangeably to refer to both bishops (3:1) and deacons (3:8). In short, the story of elders in Judeo-Christian teaching emphasized reverence, responsibility, and privilege. Titus 1:5 reads: "I left you on the island of Crete so you could complete our work there and appoint elders in each town as I instructed you." Interestingly, the concept of retirement is unknown in the Bible and other early literature. Elders persist in essential roles such as assisting younger priests (Numbers 8:24–26) and continuing temple service (Luke 1:18–25).

Reverence for old age is also an ancient tenet of Islam. In Islamic anthropology, old age is divided into two periods: *Mobkerah*, which goes from sixty to seventy years of age, and *Moteakherah* (meaning "senile"), which is seventy until the end of life. Old age in Islam is highly valued, as illustrated by Prophet Muhammad's view that "whenever one is in the presence of a senile in the tribe, respect him. There are three types of people to whom no one shows disrespect (except for the person whose hypocrisy is manifest): the white-bearded, the just leader, and the teacher of virtues. To have people of old age will increase the mercy and the beneficence of God on him/her and will expand one's blessings unto him/her."[1] Islamic verses also emphasize the concept of filial piety, cementing the ethical and moral responsibility of generational respect. "And your Lord has decreed that you worship none but Him. And that you be dutiful to your parents. If one or both of them attain old age in your life, say not to them a word of disrespect, nor shout at them but address them in terms of honor" (17:23).

During ancient times, older people assumed roles as teachers, healers, and historians. They were known to be keepers of vital knowledge essential to survival, such as the locations of water holes and edible versus poisonous plants and other foods. In early gerontocratic societies, elders held positions of power predicated on their accumulation of life experiences. Knowledge of lineage and familial relationships that elders possessed often formed the basis of sharing resources. Examples abound from ancient societies like Egypt, China, Greece, and India of the worth ascribed to older people. In ancient Egypt, the attainment of old age was seen as a reward earned by living a balanced and virtuous life. In ancient China, reverence and respect for older people manifested itself through an emphasis on interdependent familial relations between young and old over the quest for personal independence.[2] Also, ancestral worship was the foundation of ancient Chinese religious beliefs, a practice that ensured that a respected elder's high status would transition into ancestorhood.[3]

In *The Analects*, Confucius praises the cycle of aging as a journey that takes us closer to the divine and into our own hearts: "At 15 I set my heart on learning, at 30 I knew where I stood, at 40 I had no more doubts, at 50 I knew the will of Heaven [life's purpose], at 60 my hearts were attuned [moral sense was developed] and at 70 I followed my heart's desire without crossing the line" (2:4). Confucius also spoke of the value and responsibility of filial piety, positioning old age as worthy of dignity, respect, and authority. As stated in volume 3 of *The Chinese Classics*:

> The Master said, "(It was filial piety.) Now filial piety is the root of (all) virtue, and (the stem) out of which grows (all moral) teaching . . . Our bodies — to every hair and bit of skin — are received by us from our parents, and we must not presume to injure or wound them. This is the beginning of filial piety. When we have established our character by the practice of the (filial) course, so as to make our name famous in future ages, and thereby glorify our parents: — this is the end of filial piety. It commences with the service of parents; it proceeds to the service of the ruler; it is completed by the establishment of the character."[4]

In Hindu teaching, the ethical-legal texts known as the Dharma-sastras (200–100 BCE) describe how people move through a series of four life stages known as *ashramas*: as a chaste student (*brahmacharya*), a householder (*grihastha*), a forest-dweller (*vanaprastha*) starting to disengage, and a wandering ascetic renouncer (*sannyasa*).[5] The two latter stages include a release from the pleasure and ties of the physical world and focus on God and spiritual discovery, a concept that thousands of years later is referred to in the gerontology field as gerotranscendence.[6]

In ancient Rome in 44 BCE, Cicero wrote in his famous essay *On Old Age*: "The arms best adapted to old age are the attainment and practice of the virtues; if cultivated at every period of life these produce wonderful fruits when you reach old age." Cicero offered his own conceptualization of the stages of life: "Life has its fixed course, and nature one unvarying way; to each is allotted its appropriate quality, so that the fickleness of boyhood, the impetuosity of youth, the sobriety of middle life, and the ripeness of age all have something of nature's yield which must be garnered in its own season."[7]

In the fifteenth century, the Puritans embraced the biblical conception of life as a journey, and aging was seen as part of a continuous process of progress toward salvation. Aging and spirituality were tightly interwoven into the fabric of societal ideals. Respect for old age and end of life can be seen in a poem from the 1600s by Anne Bradstreet titled "Of the Four Ages of Man":[8]

> And last of all to act upon this stage
> Leaning upon his staff came up Old Age,
> Under his arm a sheaf of wheat he bore,
> An harvest of the best, what needs he more?
> In's other hand a glass ev'n almost run,
> This write about: This out then I am done,
> His hoary hairs, and grave aspect made way,
> And all gave ear to what he has to say.

Old as Diseased

A perspective on aging and oldness contrary to the one presented above also existed throughout history. The Sir Edwin Smith Surgical Papyrus (2800–2700 BCE) contains the earliest known recorded remedy for wrinkles (interestingly, an ingredient still used in modern anti-wrinkle creams): "It is a remover of wrinkles from the head. When the flesh is smeared therewith, it becomes a beautifier of the skin, remover of blemishes, of all disfigurements, of all signs of age, of all weaknesses which are in the flesh." In the margin is a note written in informal Coptic script by the scribe drawing the hieroglyphs: "Found effective myriad times."[9] This text also presents the earliest known visual reference to an older person in the form of an Egyptian hieroglyph for old age depicted by a bent-over human figure using a staff.

In ancient Greece, old age was conceptualized as a sad, downward slope of decrepitude. In *Theogony* and *Works and Days*, Hesiod (700s BCE) wrote of a "sorrowful old age" and described the unleashing of Pandora's evils of "illness and age."[10] The Greeks developed theories about causes of aging in the period of 775 BCE until 145 BCE. The Hippocratic texts highlighted the susceptibility to disease in advanced age and the very old as the least healthy people.[11] Aristotle theorized that aging was due to a loss of life force (*pneuma*), and Homer frequently emphasized that with aging came waning strength and physical debilitation.[12] To the Greeks, youth was generally regarded as the ideal state of being, sentiments that were also evident in ancient Rome. Galen, a Roman physician, described aging as a gradual loss of function and vitality through the extinction of the body's vital heat and marked by "increased desiccation."[13]

During the Middle Ages (500–1500 CE), influential scholar and friar Roger Bacon wrote in *The Cure of Old Age, and Preservation of Youth* of the pathology of aging — "like a disease" — and suggested pathways to promote longevity such as good rest, exercise, and proper diet.

When longevity gradually increased during the early Renaissance era, Gabriele Zerbi, an Italian physician, wrote the first geriatrics book, *Gerontocomia* (1499), describing mechanisms to slow aging. In the 1500s, French surgeon Ambroise Paré subdivided human life into four periods: puerility, adolescence, youth and virility, and old age. Old age was then subdivided into two parts (from thirty-five to forty-nine, and fifty years and older) and three phases: (1) some manly virtues maintained; (2) imbecility of virtues; and (3) extreme imbecility, impatience, and reversion to a second childhood.[14]

The rise of science and technology also contributed to a decreasing of the value placed on older people. The most salient example lies with the advent of the printing press. In 1440 Germany, Johannes Gutenberg developed a mechanical device that applied pressure to an inked surface, thereby transferring text with ease. The printing press was revelatory and made possible the rapid creation, distribution, and preservation of written material. Suddenly elders were no longer needed in their roles as the primary historians, storytellers, and living encyclopedias, and their status and power in the community diminished as a direct result.

These illustrations from history provide the necessary framework for understanding that attitudes about aging are complicated as well as *why*.

Aging: The Complicated Truth

Aging is a complex process. It is not just one thing but rather a series of processes that involve contradictory mechanisms happening simultaneously. As we age, we experience decline, growth, and maintenance all at once and in varying gradations.

Decline is the paradigm that we are all most familiar with because the signs and effects of physical decline are so salient in everyday life. It is easy to recognize, and we so often talk about daily aches, pains, and struggles to do the physical things we used to do with ease. Stories of decline and physical loss are shared from person to person and generation to generation, and they build both empathy and fear. Empathy is an essential human trait, and empathy exercises are often built into health profession curriculums to help connect providers with their patients.

AGNES (Age Gain Now Empathy System) is one such empathy-building exercise. Students wear a suit designed to approximate the motor skills, visual ability, flexibility, dexterity, and strength of a person in their midseventies. Results from studies with AGNES show that young adult users develop empathy that results in better future innovation and designs for older people.[15] There are certainly benefits to using technology to provide context, build empathy, and spark ideas for innovation. That said, I believe having empathy as a central focus of instruction is a misguided, limited, and frankly perilous approach.

Empathy is a term used to describe understanding and sharing another's feelings. The problem with this aging suit is that while it does an excellent job of allowing the user to "walk a mile in another's shoes" *physically*, it does nothing to contextualize the experience with the growth and development that come with age and balance the sense of loss older adults feel. Simulating aging in this manner can provoke cognitive dissonance by simultaneously invoking competing feelings of empathy and fear. No simulation suit can capture an older adult's mind-set and emotions. For example, the suit cannot grasp the age-related trend known as the positivity effect.[16] As described by Laura Carstensen, we become more skilled as we grow older at recognizing and attending to positive emotions and memories, whereas negative-oriented material is more likely to come to the fore among younger people. Older people are more likely to report excellent self-rated health despite their physical limitations. Having a younger person who has not yet developed the skills and maturity to understand an older person's sense of comfort with their own bodies wear a suit to mimic aging is shortsighted and dangerous.

The Botswanan concept of *botsofe* (old age) can help illustrate the danger of a one-dimensional experience like an aging suit. *Botsofe* suggests a "complex state in which physical infirmity, spiritual potency, and aggregated knowledge and experience converge in an individual near the end of a long life."[17] Accordingly, "physiology itself is never the total measure of age, rather it reminds the observer of the potential for cultural authority, knowledge, spiritual transcendence, proximity to ancestors, political capital, and position within the family."[18] Simulation mechanisms to build empathy, while well intended, are deeply limited by the inability to capture how knowledge, experience, spirituality, and robust protective cognitive factors influence the experience of aging. Aging is more than changes to our bodies. Aging is a process of change, adaptation, and growth.

There are indeed normal and expected effects of becoming older on the body. These include changes to hair (which gets thinner and turns gray), eyesight (lenses harden, yellow, and lose transparency), hearing (ability to hear high-frequency sounds diminishes), skin (becomes less elastic and thinner), and bones (become less dense, and cartilage breaks down). There are also pathological processes that are more likely to occur as we age, such as developing arthritis or a heart or vascular condition. Notice that I say more likely, not guaranteed. Certain aspects of biological aging are universal, but more factors are idiosyncratic and depend on genes, individual behavior, and environment. However, the nature of physical change with aging is a universal connector — something we can talk about, share with each other, and understand. Perhaps this commonality is why we are so quick to think of physical decline first when we think about aging.

Nigerian writer Chimamanda Ngozi Adichie eloquently describes the hazard of making judgments based on limited knowledge in her TED Talk, "The Danger of a Single Story." Adichie's claim that stereotypes aren't necessarily untrue but always incomplete is a salient point related to the story of aging. What we know, what we talk about, and what we model and teach each other is the single story of aging as physical decline. What we lack is a story that captures the rich, nuanced complexities of the aging experience taken as a whole.

Let me illustrate by asking a question. Think for a moment about a younger version of you. What comes to mind? Is it a vision of an energetic, active, risk-taking person with few fears or cares? Is it an awkward, unsure, immature person who lacked self-confidence and self-esteem? For many, these would both be accurate and valid assessments. Aging is no different. It involves things lost and also things gained, and this is the story less told.

Intelligence provides a perfect example of the complexity of simultaneous loss and gains with aging. Fluid and crystallized intelligence changes over time, with particular abilities peaking at different points in the life span. Fluid intelligence, the ability to solve problems in new situations without preexisting knowledge, is known to decline as we age. Crystallized intelligence, the ability to use previously acquired knowledge through education and experience, continues to increase with age. When the same construct — intelligence — is assessed two different ways, we see contradictory results of growth and decline. To make matters more complicated, we also know that the perceived reduction in fluid intelligence with age dissipates or disappears altogether when attentional factors like concentration and perceptual speed are also taken into account.[19] The mitigation of decline in fluid intelligence exemplifies yet another salient aspect of aging — adaptation.

Research demonstrates that those who experience aging as a lifelong journey are more likely to feel that their later years consist of renewal and engagement. In other words, a sense of the whole journey is essential to optimal adaptation to elderhood. This is illustrated by the U curve of happiness, a striking and somewhat surprising concept for many people. This U curve demonstrates that happiness declines with age from early adolescence to midlife and then turns upward and increases with advanced age. Research has shown this concept to be pan-cultural — it held in forty-four out of forty-six countries studied.[20]

Anti-ageism begins with the recognition that aging involves both challenges and opportunities. Understanding the complexity of aging as simultaneous processes of growth, decline, and adaptation underscores ancient Chinese views and calls into question the dominant ancient Greek views on aging. Both perspectives were informed by valid interpretations of aging. It cannot be denied that the process of aging includes many negative experiences along with the positive ones — but that is the case for every stage of life! Embracing the complexity and the nuances of holistic aging is the first step to dismantling ageism and creating an anti-ageist frame of mind.

CHAPTER TWO

The Era of Technology and Medicine

*The charm of history and its enigmatic lesson consist in
the fact that, from age to age, nothing changes and yet
everything is completely different.*

— ALDOUS HUXLEY

M y family tells a story from time to time about my nonny and a CD player. In the 1980s, my grandparents purchased a CD player for the first time. Being music aficionados, they excitedly anticipated how this new technology would bring better quality of sound to their favorite classical music. My father purchased some CDs and dropped them off at their house. Later that afternoon, he got a call from Nonny telling him that she could not get the CD player to work. Nonny described with some frustration how the CD would not fit into the designated slot — it was simply too big. Upon questioning her, my father determined that she had yet to take the CD out of its case and was attempting to put the CD case into the machine rather than the disc.

There are countless stories like this one from families, told with laughs and good humor. At the same time, this story is also a brick in the foundation of ageist stereotypes about older people being left behind in a modernized society.

There is a broad misconception that older people and technology don't mix. This generalization is based on several perceived truths, such as that older people are not interested in using technology, find technology to be unnecessary, and don't understand how to interact with technology — as well as the infamous (and incorrect) saying that "you can't teach an old dog new tricks." Some older people certainly have reservations and challenges with technology (as do younger people); however, many older people adopt new technology willingly and excitedly. Yet the myth of older people as the left-behind victims of a modern technological world is primarily accepted. Fault can be found in the industries themselves, which systematically exclude older people from the development, design, and marketing of new technologies. The roots of stereotypes and generalizations about older people as out of touch with technology can be traced back to the Industrial Revolution, when technology and industry drastically altered circumstances for older people and attitudes about aging.

Throughout American colonial history, older people were considered active and productive contributors to the economy and society. This changed in the late 1700s to mid-1800s when significant cultural, technological, and socioeconomic changes resulted from the development of an economy dominated by machine manufacturing. In agrarian times, elders were viewed as learned farmers, essential providers, and primary educators of future generations. It should be noted that age alone was not a guarantee of respect; wealth, race, and gender have always been determinative factors of social acceptance and value. Older white men held positions of power and authority that dictated the protection of rights, money, land, and power.

The advent of the industrial era brought new priorities; to survive in the new economy, people needed to be able to relocate quickly, to work in factories, and to adopt and adapt to new and fast-changing technology. The extended family structure suffered, and the prized role of elder changed drastically. Moving to where the jobs were was easier and more appealing for younger people. Older family members were reluctant to move away from family land, which created competing priorities for family units. In this way, the Industrial Revolution significantly affected the family structure and the value system that had existed for millennia. Tradition and stability were replaced with mobility and adaptability.[1]

With the rise of industrialization came urbanization and the increasing separation of living and working spaces. People no longer needed to live on the farms where they worked but rather preferred to live in locations separate from their workplaces. Historian Andrew Achenbaum notes that the shift to industrialization and urbanization from 1860 to 1914 marked a critical turning point in attitudes toward older people, who became widely perceived as a burden on society.[2] These shifting perceptions created destabilization and the loss of authority for many older people, most notably the poor. Older widows were especially vulnerable and dependent on others' charity within their communities. Social values dictated that older women, especially unmarried or widowed, were unemployable and therefore economically unable to maintain independent living. To accommodate the "neediness" of such people, public relief was provided in an almshouse, also known as the poorhouse. The proliferation of almshouses, accompanied by changes to family structure, during the nineteenth century caused a sharp decline in multigenerational family households and a resulting increase in older people needing public assistance. Simultaneously, asylums were built to deal with those deemed as "less able" due to mental illness and physical disability. A reform movement got under way lobbying for poor children, also residing in almshouses and asylums, to be relocated to more suitable environments.[3] The result was the beginning of a long and continued history of segregation of old people, frail people, and people with cognitive and physical disabilities.

Segregation of the Old and Disabled

The normalization of segregating the old and disabled represents a significant marker in the development of structural ageism and a considerable shift in thinking about the roles and responsibilities of caregiving. Structural ageism excludes or deprioritizes specific age cohorts through laws, policies, and practices.[4] It also incorporates ageist principles into formal and informal rules and procedures. Structural ageism is reflected in the legal system, health care provisions, economic practices, and the built environment. Age limits, health care access prioritization based on age, and the lack of widely available environmental supports — things like ramps, ADA accessible facilities, and appropriate lighting — are all types of structural ageism. If you have ever dined at a restaurant with hard-to-read menus in minuscule font sizes, poorly lit and with distracting music and ambient noise in the background, you have experienced structural ageism and ableism. Regardless of age, those with any sensory challenges would find themselves at a disadvantage in this type of environment.

In the nineteenth century, caregiving occurred primarily in the home and was confined to a relatively short duration due to a lack of medical knowledge and of interventions to extend the average life span. The proliferation of facilities external to the home where nurses provided long-term care shaped the social milieu for informal and formal caregiving. The term *caregiving* wasn't noted until 1966, when the terminology to distinguish between unpaid care (informal caregivers) and paid care (formal caregivers) was established.[5] Both formal and informal caregiving encompass the act of providing help and support to individuals who are unable to function independently. Interestingly, within the family context, the expectation of providing care for children remained intact, and we view parenthood as a responsibility that encompasses both challenges and great rewards. However, caregiving for older family members became regarded as a constraint and associated with a burden as time went on.

The social construction of childhood that became widely adopted in the early twentieth century exacerbated the split between how we think about caregiving for children and for older people. Previously, children typically had been tasked with substantive work responsibilities and treated as economic contributors to the family. When the economic landscape no longer necessitated this practice, society's idea of childhood evolved. It became identified as a stage in which to grow, play, learn, and develop in supported and protected environments. This new social construction of childhood also advanced the understanding of aging itself as a rise in ability and vitality from childhood into adulthood followed by a slow and steady decline into old age.

With an increased emphasis on childcare as a familial obligation came an increased reliance on paid caregivers for elders. Caregiving in recent decades has come to imply a one-way relationship between someone who actively gives care and someone who passively receives it. The concept of the caregiver's burden emerged in the 1960s and effectively pathologized the caring relationship. This in turn added to the stigma of dependence and promoted the illusion of autonomy as the goal of successful aging. Who wants to be a burden? I have heard numerous conversations in which an elder expressed fear of encumbering a loved one through dependency. Bioethicist Ezekiel Emanuel even wrote an essay for *The Atlantic* in 2014 making the case that we'd all be better off if people promptly died at seventy-five before becoming a burden on society and family members. Emanuel's writing had its share of satire and hyperbole to be sure, but his disdain for support and fear of dependency was crystalline. We need to ask ourselves why we are so terrified and uncomfortable receiving and asking for help from others.

Of course, relying directly on others every day can elicit feelings of vulnerability, frustration, and weakness for both the care provider and the care recipient. However, the care process can also evoke warmth, connection, trust, purpose, and love. Providing care to others can be a rich and gratifying experience that encourages meaningful relationships built upon interdependence. It wasn't until the 1990s that research began to focus on caregiving's positive aspects with concepts such as caregiver satisfaction and caregiver rewards. Ending this pattern and healing damage already done starts by recognizing the stigma currently associated with dependence and the concurrent misconception of independence as an attainable goal. This false dichotomy then must be replaced with an appreciation of the reciprocity involved in giving and receiving care as a healthy relational process.

Not surprisingly, cultural expectations dictated that caring for family members was central to a woman's self-sacrificing service to her children, husband, and parents.[6] To care for others was deemed women's work, and the selfless obligation to care for others was seen as a poignant embodiment of female virtue.[7] During the nineteenth century, nursing became synonymous with caring as the Civil War erupted and women volunteered, and the nursing profession evolved from a job performing domestic duties to one that encompassed patient treatment. Nursing transitioned to a private-sector job as the growing middle and upper classes had money to pay women to care for relatives within the home. The transition to segregated facilities for housing and caring for the old and disabled further solidified nursing as a paid profession and accelerated movement away from traditional intergenerational family care to the relegation of responsibility for looking after older people to paid caregivers.

Systematically the almshouses that accompanied industrialization and urbanization transformed into "homes for the elderly," creating the perfect storm of social and economic changes to cement discriminatory ageist practices and policies. We slowly began to view older people as *others* — pitiable, weak, irrelevant, and separate. Older people, especially those with physical, cognitive, or psychological vulnerabilities, started to become warehoused away from those of us regarded by society as productive and independent. Yet as people experienced their living environments drastically changing, we forgot to ask the most important question of all: Is this what older people wanted?

Given that we have no survey data from the time of the Industrial Revolution, we can only speculate that older people were no
more in favor of being segregated back then than they are today.
Recent findings from the United States of Aging National Survey
show that nine of ten older adults strive to remain living in their
homes and communities despite physical or economic difficulties.[8]
The most prevalent reasons for wanting to stay in their homes is
that they like where they live and have friends nearby. It should not
be shocking to think that older people, like people of other ages,
would prefer to have the autonomy, agency, and ability to live
where and how they wish and to be among the people they know.
The physical separation of older people from the rest of society has
been a significant driver in the development of rampant, unchecked
discrimination against the old and disabled — ageism and ableism.

The Twins Were Born: Ageism and Ableism

The systematic devaluing of older people that has been interwoven
into the fabric of our culture since the Industrial Revolution was
not described by the term *ageism* until Robert Butler coined it in
1969. Subtle shifts in the language used to discuss productivity and
profits in the job market, however, pointed to changes that were
becoming endemic, such as the new practice of "retiring" older
workers from their positions, a practice sold to the American public
as beneficial.[9] From 1880 forward, a substantive shift in language
that advanced age stereotypes grew exponentially as the term
elderly became equated with frailty. Terms like *efficient* became
code for "young" — a practice that exists to this day — as this
excerpt from 1913 illustrates:

In the search for increased efficiency, begotten in modern
time by the practically universal worship of the dollar . . .
gray hair has come to be recognized as an unforgiving

witness of industrial imbecility, and experience, the invari-
able companion of advancing years, instead of being valued as common sense would require it to be, has become
a handicap so great as to make the employment of its pos-
sessor, in the performance of tasks and duties for which
life work has fitted him, practically impossible.[10]

The language of disability also normalized in the 1900s when
terms like *handicapped* were used to describe people who were seen
as defective. *Handicapped* became associated with social, economic,
and physical disadvantages, and terms like *cripple* or *lame* were used
as pejoratives. The language of ableism can be traced back to the
beliefs and practices of the pseudoscience of eugenics.[11] The 1883
book *Inquiries into Human Faculty and Its Development*, by Sir Francis
Galton, whose cousin was Charles Darwin, popularized the term
eugenics. Although *eugenics* means "good creation," the concept is
built on the belief that the human species can be improved by
selectively breeding out disease, disability, and other undesirable
characteristics from the human population by mating people with
desirable hereditary characteristics.[12] The first known appearance
of government-sanctioned eugenics in the United States occurred
in 1896 when Connecticut passed a law decreeing that those with
epilepsy or who were considered feeble-minded were not legally
allowed to marry. The concept gained traction in the early twentieth century, resulting in forced sterilizations of those with mental
illness, physical and mental disabilities, and racial and ethnic
minority status. Today we use the term *ableism* to describe a set of
beliefs and practices that places value and judgment on physical,
cognitive, and intellectual ability. As with ageism, we are aware that
the preference for particular abilities over others leads to oppression and marginalization and ultimately "othering" of people
deemed less capable.

It wasn't until the latter twentieth century that concerted efforts
were made to clarify the weighty stigma intrinsic to these terms

and to provide alternatives to the term *handicapped*, such as *disabled* or *differently abled*. The rise of the eugenics movement and the biomedicalization of aging equated *disabled* and *old* with inferiority and social problems. Negative attitudes and behaviors toward disability and advanced age became more mainstream, driven by concerns that older people were a drain on economic resources.

Advances in technology and medicine had led to a demographic explosion. The proportion of the US population that was described as elderly burgeoned from 4 percent in 1900 to 10 percent in 1950. Moreover, the oldest of the old, those over seventy-five, made up the fastest-growing group, with the percentage of the older population that was living alone, primarily women, increasing from 10 percent to 36.[13] Meanwhile, the working-age population was shrinking, compounding concerns over the growing financial costs associated with more people living longer. A reduction in the average family size and an exodus of young adults from family farms to cities contributed to anxiety over who would provide medical and personal care to the old. These changing demographics spurred catastrophic language describing the aging population as an "impending disaster."

Aging: A Single View of Decline and Withdrawal

The Industrial Revolution birthed the start of a longevity revolution as advances in medicine and technology began to influence a rapid rise in average life expectancy. In 1900 average life expectancy in the United States was 47.3 years of age, and by 2000 it was 76.8.[14] Technological advances that improved sanitation and health care and sharply decreased the incidence of infant mortality were significant drivers of growing life expectancy. But the development of the smallpox vaccine by Edward Jenner in 1798 played perhaps the greatest role.[15] Other vaccinations followed in the wake of the triumph over smallpox, as did a range of other medications. Fluorinated water, a focus on nutrition, safety practices, and modern heating and refrigeration extended the longevity trend with safer and healthier home and work environments. The early twentieth century also formalized medicine's biomedical model, the dominant model driving advancements in health for the century that followed.

The biomedical model views health as the absence of disease, infirmity, and disability, focusing on curative solutions. Maintaining ecological balance among three factors — the human body, the environment, and pathogens — was understood as the key to good health. The biomedical model became the dominant framework for shaping our understanding of aging and disability. Disability, and therefore aging by proxy, was viewed as the result of pathology, impairment, or dysfunction of the body. This view spurred the medicalization of aging and disability, circulating the damaging narratives that enabled ageist and ableist thoughts and practices to proliferate.

The biomedical model was endorsed as the gold standard of medical training by Abraham Flexner in 1910 when he outlined his vision for the future of academic medical education in what became known as the Flexner Report. Flexner's work was incredibly influential, resulting in the transformation of medical educational institutions. Although Flexner embraced educational methods focused on scientific knowledge, he built upon his "infatuation with the hyper-rational world of German medicine which created excellence in science that was not balanced by a comparable excellence in clinical caring."[16] The biomedical approach heralded scientific understanding of the development, diagnosis, and treatments of specific disease states, leading to incredible advances in medical technology. However, the biomedical model was reductionist with its approach to health as the absence of disease, to disease as the precursor to symptoms and illness, and to symptoms and illness as indicators of an underlying abnormality.

This simplistic view saw old age as a process of inevitable, immutable biological phenomena whereby normal aging encompasses decline, disability, degeneration, and death. Of course, the processes of physical decline — senescence — are embedded within the totality of the aging process. We are mortal beings and will all eventually decline and die. However, aging and dying are distinctly different processes. Dying is gradually ceasing to exist or function; aging is living, evolving, and growing. So classifying aging (or even more powerfully, classifying normal aging) firmly within the biomedical framework as decline, degeneration, and death ignored the holistic and multidirectional paradox of aging and encouraged pathologizing aging as a medical problem.

The emergence of the biomedical model meant that growing older was something to be treated. As the focus on curative medicine increased, older and disabled people were often dismissed as a lost cause not worth treating. Although this transition occurred a century ago, these narratives continue to have a colossal impact today.

The view of aging as a medical problem had consequences for the overall shaping of the discipline of medicine, from research to training to the structures and missions of organizations.[17] Perhaps most importantly, the biomedicalization of aging profoundly shaped public perception. Aging was officially socially constructed as a medical problem to be diagnosed, treated, and managed. As a result, medical advances capitalized on extending physical life without fully addressing the cost and quality of life associated with longevity.[18] The biomedical model also failed to acknowledge the social factors that contribute to systemic health and disparities in longevity, and it ignored the environment's influence on health and well-being.

We now recognize the importance of social factors and policies and understand that they are inextricably linked to health outcomes. *Social determinants of health* — SDOH — is the term used to describe how people's environments affect overall sickness, life expectancy, and longevity. The concept of SDOH is simple: Health starts in our homes, schools, and jobs. Health is affected by housing, transportation, the walkability of neighborhoods, education, access to healthy food, access to health care, social support, and the impact of discrimination and stress. Therefore, the opportunities for healthy aging and longevity are shaped in large part by our families, neighborhoods, and all of the external systems that we count on to get the things we need. Without access to safe housing, adequate health care, and healthy food, disadvantages accumulate over the years and disproportionately affect people already at risk, such as people of color and women. As a result of a lifetime of deprivation due to poverty, systemic racism and sexism, lack of equal opportunity, and historical and generational trauma, inequities accrue and have adverse long-term effects. This intersectionality, or cumulative discrimination, is exacerbated further as disenfranchisement based on racial and gender identity combine with age oppression. The absence of recognition within the biomedical model that systems of inequality contribute to the outcomes of aging was a perilous oversight with far-reaching consequences.

The biomedical model was most effective at problematizing aging and disability; even the first US gerontological handbook, *Cowdry's Problems of Aging*, couched aging as a conundrum rather than a normal and natural part of the life course.[19] Furthermore, by not acknowledging the extent to which social factors and policy influence health and longevity, the biomedical model perpetuated a misconstruction of healthy aging as a product of individual behavior and choices. Personal, rather than collective, responsibility for aging was exacerbated further by the fact that during the nineteenth century two schools of thought had emerged to transform ideals of sickness and bodily health.

In that era, the social purity movement, driven by the tenets of Christian morality, was formed to end prostitution and sexual activities considered immoral. Progressive-era reformers founded the social hygiene movement late in the century to emphasize bodily health as a way to regulate prostitution further and control the spread of venereal disease. These movements transformed popular ideas of disease, sickness, and death, which became "the price of moral transgression and ungodliness."[20] Decline, disability, and death were regarded as failures of the individual due to poor self-care practices and questionable morality. Popular advice literature in the nineteenth century reinforced this narrative and cemented the individualist notion that a good old age, achievable through self-control, was disease-free, whereas a bad old age encompassed the harsh realities of decline. At the time, scientific and medical practice lacked a framework to study and treat diseases of old age and classified and diagnosed those as being afflicted with old age as untreatable.

Meanwhile, a countereffort was under way that recognized the need to develop medical approaches to combat disease and alleviate suffering for older people.[21] A new medical specialty to treat older age was named in the early 1900s when Ignatz Nascher, a New York physician, created the word *geriatrics* by combining the Greek words *geron* (old man) and *iatrikos* (medical treatment).[22] Unlike his contemporaries, Nascher refused to accept a widely held dismissive view that old age was a syndrome that could not be treated. But a British surgeon, Marjory Warren, is considered the mother of geriatric medicine. In the 1940s, Warren advocated for creating a medical specialty focused on the needs and rehabilitation of older people and educating medical students about the care of older people. Warren's vision provided the seminal theoretical underpinnings of modern geriatrics, which flourished as an interdisciplinary field over the next seventy years.[23]

Despite enormous advances in research and practice, the specialty of geriatric medicine remains one of the least favored areas by medical students. As the population of older people continues to grow and as people live longer while experiencing chronic conditions, the need for professionals trained in geriatrics is at an all-time high. Yet there is currently a critical shortage. The most commonly cited reason? Medical students prefer young patients who can be cured.[24]

Ageism in Health Care

Older adults represent the foremost consumers of health care services worldwide, yet negative attitudes and behaviors toward older patients persist across health care settings and among medical professionals.[25] An in-depth exploration of ageism within the health care system is beyond this book's scope; nevertheless, a synopsis is essential to understanding the breadth and depth of the issue and the effect it has today. Robert Butler, who coined the term, aptly stated that ageism results from stereotypes of older people being "categorized as senile, rigid, and old-fashioned in morality and skills. Ageism allows those of us who are younger to see old people as 'different.' We subtly cease to identify with them as human beings, which enables us to feel more comfortable about our neglect and dislike of them."[26]

The reasons for ageism in health care are varied and complex, and there is ample evidence that medical personnel, including doctors and nurses, commonly hold negative attitudes toward older patients. One possible explanation revolves around an idea called terror management theory, which postulates that humans have an innate ego-protective mechanism to separate themselves from the negative aspects of old age.[27] According to this theory, ageism would result from older people being a constant reminder of one's mortality and vulnerability. This is particularly salient for medical professionals exposed to the most vulnerable and frail older people and can lead directly to othering those in their care who provoke deep-seated fears. Other explanations for the high prevalence of ageism among health care professionals include a desire to focus on curative medicine; the complexities of evaluating, diagnosing, and managing multiple comorbidities; and a systematic focus on efficiency and productivity concerning reimbursement rates and payments. Moreover, the roots of ageism within health care are deeply embedded in the health care system itself and extend broadly from the training medical professionals receive to the health care policies that dictate their practices.

Since the 1980s, tremendous progress has been made incorporating specific geriatrics training into medical education. In 2007, the Association of American Medical Colleges (AAMC) and the John A. Hartford Foundation facilitated developing core competencies in geriatric domains for medical school curriculums. Yet despite the tremendous need for practitioners and the growing population of older people, interest in geriatrics as a specialization continues to wane. One reason for this lack of interest is an inadvertent hidden curriculum that enculturates medical students' bias against older people.[28] The hidden curriculum represents the socialization process whereby medical students learn through communication and patient interactions modeled by preceptors. This is where the rubber meets the road in learning about how to be a physician. In the training process, explicit bias toward older people is modeled through therapeutic nihilism, reliance on stereotypes for therapeutic decision-making, and interpersonal interactions infantilizing or demeaning older people. In a novel that offered an unvarnished view of medical training, *House of God*, Samuel Shem popularized dismissive medical terminology referring to older patients, such as *Gomer* (get out of my emergency room), *spos* (semi-human piece of shit), and *LOL in NAD* (little old lady in no apparent distress).[29] In practical terms, language shapes attitudes that translate into age dictating access to treatment, a view of older people as beyond help and too complicated to warrant diagnosis, and failures to comprehensively investigate patient histories. Ageist biases may lead medical professionals and older patients to believe that pain and suffering are expected aspects of old age. This nihilist attitude diminishes opportunities for older people to seek treatments to improve their quality of life.

Socialization in medical training is a powerful influence that should not be underestimated. A 2001 study demonstrated that patterns of treatment recommendations vary solely based on age. In this study, physicians and medical students were provided with two hypothetical cases of women with breast cancer that were identical

— except for the patient's age.[30] When asked to provide treatment recommendations, students were more likely to recommend the fictitious younger patients for the more aggressive therapy, whereas they recommended the modified and more conservative treatment for the older patients. Age alone dictating medical decision-making is highly problematic and frankly unethical, given that we know age alone is not a good indicator of health status or ability to recover.

Another contributing factor to ageism in health care can be found in the interpersonal dynamics of the physician–patient relationship, where older people are more commonly left out of the decision-making process. I cringe when I think about how many conversations I have witnessed in which a medical professional doesn't directly address an older person. Several years ago, my dad was having back pain that limited his ability to walk long distances. On one sunny, warm summer day, my family decided to take an outing to a festival to enjoy the weather and the activities. We knew we were taking a chance with my dad walking from the parking lot to the venue, but we risked it. As we were making our way through the crowd, the searing back pain became too intense for my dad to continue and we had to stop. Only there was nowhere to sit. So he sat on the ground, propped against a cement pillar.

When a well-meaning attendant approached us to see if my dad was okay, he looked directly at me as he inquired about my dad's well-being. My dad was literally right there next to me. When I suggested that the kind man address my father directly, he asked him, "Are you okay?" in a slow, loud, and over-enunciated manner. *Elderspeak* is a term used to describe the characteristic slower, louder, simplified, and patronizing speech used when communicating with an older person. Elderspeak isn't just infantilizing and demeaning, it's also disempowering for the receiver and it reinforces other-directed and self-directed ageism. Someone shouting sweetie, honey, or dear as if you can't hear or understand doesn't do much for self-esteem or confidence. Neither does a medical professional speaking to the person who accompanies the older person to an appointment rather than to the patient directly. Such ageist interactions can act as a deterrent for older people to seek treatment at all.

Older patients are not the only ones at risk; health care professionals are at risk themselves. Ageism is internalized, and stereotypes can become a self-fulfilling prophecy. Negative self-directed ageism, which has long-term consequences for personal health and functioning, is a process called stereotype embodiment.[31] Once a stereotype is accepted as truth, it becomes part of our implicit beliefs. Damaging and limiting ageist assumptions follow us throughout our lives and eventually become part of our reality. We become what we see and what we believe. This internalization process is a contagion that continually perpetuates the cycle. Health care professionals are at higher risk of internalizing ageism. They are consistently exposed to the frailest and most vulnerable population of older people, which in turn creates disproportionality among older role models.

Age discrimination in health care is also institutionally mandated within laws, policies, and practices, as evidenced by a lack of prioritization and support for geriatrics training. In 2006, $31.5 million in funding for geriatrics training and education was stripped entirely by the US Congress in the Labor–Health and Human Services appropriations bill.[32] The Medicare system for providing medical insurance for older people in America has different reimbursement rates for medications and services from those private insurance provides to younger people. Medicare reimbursement policies do not cover many preventive services or part-time support services to help older people in need of minimal assistance to stay safe in their own homes. Doctors can opt not to accept Medicare and therefore not to treat many older patients. The health care system's ageist ideology erects barriers to the natural death and dying process. In his book *Being Mortal*, Atul Gawande writes:

> Modern scientific capability has profoundly altered the
> course of human life. People live longer and better than at

any other time in history. But scientific advances have
turned the process of aging and dying into medical experiences, matters to be managed by health care professionals, and we in the medical world have proved alarmingly
unprepared for it.[33]

To be anti-ageist is to recognize aging as an opportunity. This
begins with the admission that aging itself is not a problem and old
people are not a burden; instead, ageism is the self-made obstacle
to a rich and vibrant aging experience. As fallible and fragile
humans, we can shed the cloak of shame we hold so dear that it
keeps us locked into fears of dependency. An authentically anti-
ageist and anti-ableist world does not fear dependency but embraces
vulnerability. Each one of us will need assistance and will be called
upon at some point to assist. This does not represent weakness but
rather a strength of caring, nurturing, and loving human beings. If
we can let go of the myth that we are always in control — we are
not — it becomes easier to let go of the self-imposed shame that
inhibits us from reaching out to others for comfort, support, and
help. Humans are social creatures; therefore, we are inextricably
interdependent by design. Recognizing interdependence as a
dynamic state of mutual responsibility and cooperation builds a
strong foundation for healthy aging and healthy relationships.

CHAPTER THREE

Entitlements: Ageism and Ableism at Work

*Aging is an extraordinary process where you become
the person you always should have been.*

— DAVID BOWIE

P oppy was eighty-six years old when he was forced into retirement. Up until that point, he maintained a small office at the hospital and diligently (and happily) participated in rounds once a week. Poppy was in excellent health; sustaining his professional practice of medicine meant the world to him and was an integral part of his identity. He was devastated when the powers that be decided abruptly to end his professional career. They said they needed his office space. I understand the pressures the decision makers were under; structurally and institutionally, our society has been built around retirement. This is why *retired* is so widely used as another term for older adulthood.

We grow through infancy, childhood, adolescence, adulthood, and then — we retire. But what does *being retired* even mean? Merriam-Webster defines *retirement* as "withdrawal from one's position or occupation or active working life."[1] In my view, it is highly problematic that we use a term that connotes a complete withdrawal from an activity that we *used to do* to generally describe one of life's stages. Describing someone as retired says nothing about them other than they used to work. It egregiously fails to capture any relevant information about interests, passions, goals, and ambitions in the present or for the future.

Poppy's retirement was the precursor to a depression that lasted the rest of his life. The man who loved ice cream and chocolate no longer wanted either. The classical music aficionado turned down offers to listen to a CD with "No thanks, I'm retired." The professor emeritus of medicine got stripped of his identity unwillingly, and there was no structure in place to support him in an effort to find a renewed sense of purpose and meaning. Nonny was exasperated with Poppy's depression and would reach out to my father for advice. What could she do to get him to change out of his pajamas and engage with the things he loved? We all felt stuck and helpless.

Societally, we lack the understanding and the language needed to promote a path toward a meaningful elderhood. Retirement, instead, has become the primary developmental stage equated with later life. I use the term *developmental* purposefully to illustrate the absurdity. Unlike other developmental stages of life that contain meaningful milestones and markers of growth and expansion, retirement revolves around a mechanism to downshift older workers out of the workforce — sometimes with a thank-you party and a gold watch; sometimes not — and that is a big problem. Retirement is not a developmental stage; it is a social institution. The social institution of retirement was designed to provide younger workers opportunities by reducing unemployment, containing costs, and tying workers to jobs through pensions.[2] The concept of retirement also addressed older workers' needs by rewarding them for long and loyal service and providing a mechanism for older-age income security.[3] However, the formation of retirement as a social institution structurally cemented two critical notions: Being a productive and profitable worker has a time limit, and post-working life is an inevitable period of inactivity and idleness that is earned and should be desired.

Retirement as "Old Age"

It is reported that 70 percent of men sixty-five and older remained employed in America through the time of the Civil War. Landowners, predominantly men at the time, retained a great deal of authority, power, and esteem and often deeded their sons the homestead with the understanding they would receive financial and other support through their older age. However, a shift away from traditional elder authority toward control based on achievement and wealth accumulation began to get under way in the first half of the nineteenth century, and numerous documents from the period reflect a growing ambivalence toward the aged.[4]

Historians credit Augustus Caesar with conceiving the idea of retirement in 13 BCE when he created a system offering a lump-sum payment to soldiers after twenty years in a legion and five years in the military reserves.[5] Yet the social institution of retirement did not get established until the mid-1800s. The emergence of labor unions and mandatory retirement policies between 1865 and 1900 in Europe, North America, and elsewhere provided the building blocks for a retirement system. And the formal adoption of such a system, under which retirement income would be provided, first coalesced in Germany in 1889 when Chancellor Otto von Bismarck initiated the first-ever state pension system. Von Bismarck designated seventy as the age of eligibility for benefits, yet life expectancy hovered around forty-five for women and was even lower for men.[6] So retirement was designed to be a relatively small amount of money for relatively few people.

In the United States, the earliest formalized pension program was passed in 1862, but exclusively for disabled Civil War veterans or the surviving widows and orphans of soldiers who had died or been killed during active duty. In 1906, old age was added as a sufficient qualification for benefits, and more than 90 percent of remaining Civil War veterans became beneficiaries.[7] An ugly side effect of this generous system was a growing view of older men as prey for younger women looking to cash in, planting the seeds for ageist attitudes and stereotypes of older men as gullible and weak.

The American Express Company created the first private pension plan in the United States in 1875.[8] It applied to employees who had twenty years of service, had reached the age of sixty, and had been recommended by a manager and approved by a committee and also by the board of directors. This concept caught on as more and more employers started to promote efficiency and mobility and were eager to pave the way for younger workers to replace older ones. Over the next fifty years, hundreds of corporations followed suit and adopted the practice of providing an economic incentive for exiting the workforce. The Internal Revenue Act of 1921 spurred this practice further by changing the tax code to exempt employers' contributions to pensions from federal corporate income tax.[9]

In 1910, the Massachusetts Commission on Old Age Pensions defined *old* as sixty-five and older simply because sixty-five was the age already being used in most pension schemes at that time.[10] In 1916, Germany reduced its state supported retirement age from seventy to age sixty-five. In 1934, Congress passed the new federal Railroad Retirement System using sixty-five as the age for eligibility. The American Committee on Economic Security (CES) then endorsed sixty-five as a marker for retirement based on actuarial studies that demonstrated sixty-five equated to a sustainable retirement age in that it would result in a system that could be self-sustaining with modest levels of payroll taxation.[11] The Social Security Act of 1935 formally established a system for paying retired workers age sixty-five and older. And that is how sixty-five came to be regarded as the beginning of "old age."

With his support for a state pension system as a well-earned provision for retired workers, Bismarck simultaneously sent an ominous message signaling old age as a time of incapacity:

> The State must take the matter into its own hands, not as alms giving but as the right that men have to be taken care

of when, from no fault of their own, they have become unfit for work. Why should regular soldiers and officials have old-age pensions and not the soldier of labor? This thing will make its own way: it has a future.[12]

Superannuated, a commonly used term to describe people eligible for retirement during this period, provides another indication of the growing disdain for old age. It is defined as "disqualified or incapacitated by age; old and infirm . . . too old; worn out, antiquated; made out of date or obsolete, esp. by age or new developments."[13] The roots of ageist and ableist language and thought were officially planted.

Shifting demographic trends and mounting scientific studies shaped increasingly negative attitudes toward older workers. A new scientific study released in 1882 postulated that with time, parts of the body simply wore out due to age and repeated usage. This wear-and-tear theory of aging, introduced by German biologist Dr. August Weismann, was taken by many as evidence that people had a fixed capacity and time limitation for work.[14] Over the next few decades, ageism was exacerbated further with scholars, such as statistician Frederick Hoffman, claiming that ending work at sixty-five would maximize productive potential.[15] British economist William Beveridge argued that older workers lacked adaptability. Professor of medicine William Osler made the ageist decree that there was a "fixed period" for productive years from age twenty-five to forty, followed by the "uncreative years" from forty to sixty, and followed further by the unproductive useless years which commenced after sixty.[16] Osler was also one of the first to classify retirement as a time of leisure earned in the world but separate from the rest of life. All the while, the population of older people in the United States was beginning to experience a dramatic expansion. In 1900, 4.1 percent of the population was sixty-five and older. By 1950, the figure had almost doubled, to 8.1 percent.[17]

Age Discrimination: Ageism and Ableism at Work

There is an important caveat worth mentioning that speaks to the complexity of the aging experience. We do experience physical decline over time, and a high proportion of jobs during the nineteenth and the early twentieth centuries required exhaustive physical labor. So this pervasive attitude associating productivity with age was not wholly unjustified. But the phenomenon of aging was now solidly defined as a process of decline and inability, and the societal solution deemed most efficacious was to create a normalized system of withdrawal based on age. This broad misunderstanding persists to this day, and we continue to conflate age and ability.

Two terms illustrate the difficulty of using age as a sole indicator of ability and thereby occupational qualification: chronological age and functional age. *Chronological age* is age measured from birth. *Functional age* surmises an individual's age based on their functional ability. While the notion of functional age moves conceptually in a positive direction by tying age to actual ability, it is still problematic in that it attempts to explain what it means to be of a certain age. Defining what it means to be *X* years old is impossible given the complexity and multidirectionality of the aging experience. Think about it: What does it mean to be forty years old? Sixty years old? Eighty years old? Is there a universal way to categorize and classify this? The answer is indisputably no. Someone at the age of eighty-five can demonstrate physical strength and prowess, while someone at the age of forty-five can demonstrate physical weakness and frailty. Age simply cannot be a sole indicator of health and potential, no matter how it is defined.

Older age, unlike childhood, has very few normed processes that can be used as developmental milestones. In childhood, we have a plethora of checklists and charts that outline social, emotional, communication, cognitive, and physical developmental tasks, like taking the first step, mimicking sounds, and pedaling a bicycle. In childhood, these are normed, meaning that we expect these abilities to happen in a progressive and relatively predictable way. In many ways, older age is completely counter to this predictable progression. In reality, there is evidence that as people get older they become less alike, more heterogeneous, and frankly more individual and unique to themselves.[18] Accordingly, using any definition of age as the lone indicator of one's suitability for employment is misguided and flawed; no definition should be considered a barometer of one's ability to perform any kind of work.

The Social Security Act of 1935 cemented the practice of retiring at sixty-five, which became mandatory under many private pension plans. Concurrently, the Great Depression altered the financial landscape by drastically increasing the number of older people that were poor and providing significantly fewer employment opportunities for job seekers of all ages. A combination of factors including the need to reduce the size of the labor force, the low level of benefits provided under the initial legislation, and the "retirement test" (which penalized beneficiaries for having too much earned income) created a prejudicial system designed to move older people out of the workforce.[19] Social Security benefits, which were touted as a social advancement, reinforced rather than eliminated discriminatory practices and had the practical effect of imposing enforced poverty on many older people.[20]

There has been a precipitous decline in men's labor force participation rates for those over sixty-five ever since:[21]

- 78 percent in 1880
- 65 percent in 1900
- 58 percent in 1930
- < 20 percent in 1990

Very clearly, "in a society obsessed with youth and productivity, there was no place for the older worker. Though the poor and minorities were the most heavily burdened, no class, race, ethnic group or sex were untouched by the pernicious effect of age discrimination."[22] The process of mandatory retirement became justified by the view of the aged as disabled, less efficient, less able to maintain production standards, intellectually declining, suffering decreasing stamina and strength, unable to adjust to new work situations, inflexible, and frequently absent due to illness.[23] All of which happen to be inaccurate. Of note, it wasn't until 1967 that the Age Discrimination Act was passed to protect workers forty to sixty-four who wished to remain in the workforce. Furthermore, it took until 1978 for the ADA to extend this legislation to workers up to age sixty-nine, effectively abolishing the practice of mandatory retirement before age seventy.

Let's clear up the misperceptions about older people at work with the facts:

> **Myth:** Older workers are less productive and unreliable.
>
> **Reality:** The majority of older workers can work as effectively as younger workers, with some studies showing older workers as having higher productivity.[24]
>
> **Myth:** Older workers are less motivated with less ambitious career goals.
>
> **Reality:** Older workers care about their jobs, have goals and ambitions and interest in taking on new challenges.
>
> **Myth:** Older workers are not as mentally sharp.
>
> **Reality:** Older workers bring valuable knowledge and skills to the job including higher verbal ability and knowledge from lived experience (known as crystallized intelligence).[25]
>
> **Myth:** The risk of dementia is increasing among working older Americans.
>
> **Reality:** There is evidence that the incidence of dementia is declining and has been over the past three decades.[26]
>
> **Myth:** Older workers are resistant to technology and not digitally savvy.

Reality: Countless surveys show that most older people use the internet and are more digitally connected than ever before. Research also shows that older adults are skilled at multitasking with media and technology.[27]

Myth: Older workers cost more.

Reality: Among other cost-saving benefits, older workers are more likely to remain with their employers longer, which enhances profitability.[28]

Although these myths have been debunked, negative stereotypes about older people at work have persisted, and ageist and ableist thought and practice are now profoundly institutionalized. Age discrimination in the workplace today often goes completely unnoticed. There are many ubiquitous and seemingly innocent ways it seeps into everyday organizational culture. To take stock of your organization, it can be helpful to critically examine who the learning opportunities are offered to, who is being given the challenging assignments and who is being passed over, and who is being left out of meetings or activities. If you happen to notice any age-related trends, pay attention.

If I asked you outright if age discrimination exists at your workplace, you would likely instinctively respond "no!" and offer justifiable explanations for why the types of decisions described above are made. But it is quite possible, if not likely, that underlying, unconscious motivations are driving these decisions. It is also quite possible, if not likely, that these behaviors are perceived as discriminatory by some people. Sometimes it is even the most innocent, well-intentioned, good-humored ageist behaviors that slip right by our awareness.

Have you ever been part of or witnessed a birthday party at work that has an over-the-hill theme? You might not have consciously realized it, but of course this is poking at and making fun of getting older. Celebrating another year of life with jokes about the aches, pains, and declining experiences that we equate with being "over the hill" are ageist and ableist microaggressions. A microaggression is a statement, action, or incident that is a subtle or unintentional zinger of discrimination against a person perceived as different. Ageist and ableist microaggressions are often disguised as innocuous quips, jokes, memes, emails, and offhand remarks like the following:

> "At your age, this is probably a trend that you haven't heard of . . ."
> "You are too young to remember this, but . . ."
> Saying a job applicant isn't a good "cultural fit."
> Making jokes about silly texts that your parents or grand-parents sent.
> "Your generation doesn't appreciate this . . ."
> "Happy birthday — you are old as dirt!"
> "I can't believe you have worked here for twenty years! You're a dinosaur!"

Language matters, and what seems benign can be deeply offensive; at the very least, it perpetuates ageist and ableist thoughts and behavior. It is not difficult to find words to use in your every-day conversation that don't reflect a worldview in which differently aged or differently abled people are less valued. Our quick, automatic thinking is a deterrent from identifying our language as biased or prejudicial. It is so much easier to say what is easily understood than to say what you actually mean. A simple way to check yourself is to substitute another form of identity (such as race, class, or gender) and see if you find the comment offensive. How do you feel about saying "someone of your race [or economic class or gender identity] wouldn't appreciate this . . ."? If that makes you uncomfortable, which it should, it is offensive in relation to age, too.

While we are on the topic of offensive language, it was also during the period when retirement was becoming formalized and pervasive that terms like *senior citizens* (coined in the 1930s) and *the elderly* became euphemisms for older people. These terms stigmatize older people by implying that they are a homogeneous group with common attributes like weakness, frailty, and senility. These terms condemn being old; if they didn't, why wouldn't we call younger people "junior citizens"?

Most troubling is that these ageist and ableist ideologies embedded in our language are internalized and become self-fulfilling prophecies. Becca Levy's theory of stereotype embodiment illustrates how stereotypes from the surrounding culture become internalized as negative, self-directed ageism. At work, older employees are primed to internalize the underlying beliefs and judgments expressed as microaggressions and prejudicial behaviors, such as age-based comments on their performance and potential. This internalization creates a vicious cycle whereby the myths and stereotypes of older workers that provoke age discrimination in the workplace become driving forces that perpetuate the very same behavior — a phenomenon called stereotype threat.[29]

Stereotype threat occurs when members of a marginalized group are aware that a negative stereotype exists in reference to their group and demonstrate apprehension about confirming the stereotype. That feeling of dread makes us more likely to internalize the stereotype and then display that exact behavior! Essentially, we become the stereotype, and in turn confirm it. A research study demonstrated this when older people who were told that age leads to poorer memory performed worse on a memory test than those who were told that older people perform as well as younger people.[30] We tend to care about what other people think of us, and when we feel we are being labeled and judged, we "give up and give in." This is a part of the process of relational ageism and is why we never get off the proverbial treadmill — we absorb the stereotypes, we feel devalued or unvalued, we perpetuate the stereotype, the stereotype is then confirmed and absorbed by others as truth, and the loop goes on and on.

There is an easy strategy to neutralize the impact of stereotype threat and relational ageism in the workplace: Promote positive stereotypes by encouraging diversity in teams based on age. Creating the infrastructure for people of different ages to work together and learn together is the single most cost-effective way to create an anti-ageist workplace. When people have the chance to genuinely connect with each other as authentic human beings, influential relationships develop organically and bias is challenged. An extra pro tip: Start this endeavor by having age-diverse teams spend some time discovering what they have in common with one another. You will find that, generally speaking, we tend to have a lot in common that can serve as a point of relationship bonding — no matter what ages we are.

When there is talk of "managing diversity" in the workplace, we typically focus on the much-needed work surrounding race, gender, and sexual identity and orientation, but we have yet to prioritize age and ability as important factors related to intersectionality. Yet it is undeniable from looking at history that age and ability exclusion have been interwoven into the fabric of work environments.

A Note About Generations

Another point of conflict in work environments stems from the perceived discordance among people of different generations. Until the eighteenth century, the term *generation* was used to refer to a familial generation, describing sets of relatives similar to each other in age within a line of descendants and ancestors. However, the social change resulting from industrialization and modernization sparked a youthful rebellion against the established social order. In 1863, a lexicographer named Emile Littré redefined *generation* to refer to a social construct describing all people living in society at a given point in time.[31] The concept of social generations gained in popularity, and societal divisions based on age became more prevalent. This was accompanied by political forces and movements encouraging the idea that progress and change should be driven by the power of youth. Thus, the term *generations* began to be equated with the concept of youth enfranchisement and liberation.

Karl Mannheim was the first social scientist to investigate a theory of generations and postulate that birth cohorts shared values and experiences.[32] But it was William Strauss and Neil Howe who developed our modern-day understanding of generational archetypes in their 1992 book *Generations*.[33] Generational theory posited that generational cohorts were produced by specific social and biographical experiences that created common trends in values, attitudes, and preferences. In essence, historical events and the time's zeitgeist shaped a collective personality. Generational tension, then, arises when there is discord between perceived values among people of differing generations. It has also been said that generational language and jargon contribute to misunderstanding among age cohorts.

Generational nicknames are sticky labels used to describe an entire group of people born during a specific period. Current names of generations are Traditionalists or Silent Generation (born 1945 and before), Baby Boomers (born 1946–1964), Generation X (born 1965–1976), Millennials or Gen Y (born 1977–1995), and Gen Z or iGen (born 1996–TBD). These generational labels are now commonly used to describe and predict behavioral traits.

We lump together millions upon millions of people and believe that they all have a similar blueprint of behavioral characteristics in common. For example, we regard Baby Boomers as competitive, self-disciplined, safety seeking, and good team players. We believe that the millions of individuals born in the Millennial generation feel entitled and are politically passive. I believe the concept of tying generational blueprints to behavior is total and absolute bullshit. Historical influences do not have a blanket effect on individual outcomes. Historical and cultural events shared by similarly aged people are experienced and internalized in different ways. Not only is it impossible to predict behaviors of any one individual based on date of birth, but the labeling of people within a somewhat arbitrary twenty- to thirty-year span makes no logical sense. Let me illustrate with an example. As a group, the Baby Boomers were born from 1946 to 1964. Baby Boomer A born in 1946 experienced their formative years in the 1960s, while Baby Boomer B born in 1964 lived their formative years in the 1980s. Baby Boomer A grew up in a time of the Civil Rights Movement, hippie culture, the Vietnam War, and the assassination of JFK. These were powerful cultural forces that had a strong influence on personality and identity. Baby Boomer B grew up in the 1980s and experienced the first launching of the space shuttle, the end of the Cold War, and a rise in technology, the internet, and conservative politics. Quite clearly Baby Boomer A and Baby Boomer B had very different historical events and experiences shape their development — yet we refer to them both as Baby Boomers as if they fit one mold. The same homogeneous classification system is used for every generation, and it makes absolutely no sense.

People in different generations are not as different as you might think. All generations undergo development patterns that follow similar ebbs and flows. A common head-shaking euphemism is "kids these days," but in reality, it's normal for teenagers to feel invincible and to exhibit recklessness no matter what decade they are born into. We also commonly hear "[insert generation here] is responsible for [insert grievance here]," yet the truth is that every generation has people who dedicate their time, energy, and passion to bettering the world. Regardless of the period into which people are born, they have more in common with individuals born into other generations than we are led to believe.

Pitting generations against each other kindles internalized ageism. It is no surprise that if we see older generations as wildly outdated and inept then we are likely to fear our own process of growing older. Generational labeling and stereotyping also promote other-directed ageism by perpetuating an us-versus-them mentality. Ageism results when generations see each other as *them*. Need I say more than the catchphrase and meme "OK boomer?" If you aren't familiar, "OK boomer" popped up online in 2019 and went viral as a slang phrase used to dismiss or mock attitudes ascribed to Baby Boomers. The phrase was used as commentary on political and social issues like climate change, and not surprisingly it morphed into an ageist catchall. Another form of ageism — adultism — also results from generational labels. During my ageism presentations with groups of elders, I invariably hear derogatory and dismissive comments about "those irresponsible Millennials." Remember, ageism is bidirectional. As a myth-busting side note, despite what is commonly believed about Millennials as a selfish generation, one-fourth of people providing care to elders right now are Millennials, and that number is expected to rise.[34] Just saying.

CHAPTER FOUR

Retirement as a Life Stage and Successful Aging

Aging is not lost youth but a new stage of opportunity and strength.

— BETTY FRIEDAN

My mother retired in 1999 after thirty years working as a teacher, real estate agent, independent consultant, and business owner. She and my father moved from New York to Virginia to start a new life as retirees. My father, a musician and music teacher, had plans to golf, swim, and dedicate much of his time to his love of composing and publishing music for band and orchestra. In thinking about her retirement, my mother was under the impression that her days would be spent in leisure-filled activities with my father and friends. She quickly became disillusioned when she realized that my father had a booked-up schedule with his own activities and she had absolutely nothing to do. She focused on developing a new social support system, which proved challenging. She discovered that the women she met were nested into cliques that had socialized for years. She did not want a full-time job, couldn't find a fit for a part-time job, and felt incompatible as a substitute teacher or volunteer in the local school system. She quickly discovered that the retirement she envisioned lacked not only activities but also something even more essential — purpose and meaning.

During the 1940s and '50s, the predominant view was that retirement was justifiable only for the ill or disabled. In the post–World War II era, however, as private pension plans became more prevalent and Social Security benefits were extended, retirement for all older people, regardless of ability, became viewed not only as acceptable but also as a well-earned reward for a lifetime of labor.

The Economic Opportunity Act of 1964 and the Older Americans Act of 1965 included provisions for Medicare, Medicaid, and protecting the rights of older people. Passage of the OAA in 1965 was a major legislative initiative that established the federal Administration on Aging (AoA) as well as state agencies on aging to provide services *to address the needs of* older people. I emphasize "address the needs of" quite purposefully. The OAA is a tremendously essential and influential piece of legislation that was crucial to prioritizing the needs of older people, but at the same time, it structurally defined *all* older people as vulnerable and needy. Additionally, with its well-intentioned language to help older people maintain maximum independence in their homes and communities and to promote a continuum of care for vulnerable elderly, it contributed to public discourse about ageism and ableism in two important ways. First, the language used in the legislation propagated the concept of successful aging as a state of maintaining independence. Second, it further enabled segregation based on age and ability by equating a need for care with vulnerability.

By the 1980s, a new form of large-scale age-based segregation was upon us in the form of age-restricted retirement communities. The nature of retirement evolved in the 1980s as the economics of retiring shifted from employer-defined benefit plans to individually based defined contribution plans. The onus was now on each individual to save, prepare, and plan for their own needs, moving society one step further away from the ideals of collective responsibility, as well as taking one giant leap toward intersectional inequity. Successful aging was now firmly implanted as the responsibility of the individual. The last half of the twentieth century also crystallized the idea that retirement was synonymous with older adulthood. Equating retirement with later life was pivotal to the evolution of our understanding and lack of knowledge of elderhood.

The social institution of retirement was also shaped, in part, by a deliberate and brilliant stroke of marketing the new "retirement dream" as endless, lazy, sun-soaked days filled with opportunities for relaxation and ease.

Retirement as a Life Stage

In the 1950s, the Mackle brothers began to purchase hundreds of thousands of acres of land in Florida as they devised a plan to develop subdivisions with inexpensive homes to capitalize on a new market of middle-class Americans with disposable income — retirees. The land development plan was accompanied by an aggressive nationwide marketing campaign based on the concept of retirement as a modern lifestyle with days on end of fun in the sun. The aggressive marketing outreach included running full-page ads in national periodicals, opening sales offices across the country, erecting model homes in public spaces like Grand Central Station, creating movie sets within retirement communities, and hosting lots and lots of property tours.[1] The multimillion-dollar campaign investment paid off, and demand for property in Florida surged among people from all parts of the country.[2]

The retirement dream was pitched as a carefree existence filled with amenities and access to recreation and leisure in an aesthetically pleasing tropical-like environment. And it caught on. As of 2018, Florida has the most residents aged sixty-five and older of any state, and they represent more than 20 percent of the state's total population.[3]

The Del Webb Company similarly capitalized on the retirement market and opened the first large-scale active-lifestyle age-restricted retirement community in Sun City, Arizona, in 1960. The notion of retirement as a *way of life* consisting of activity and leisure among generational peers was so popular that the grand opening created

Ad in *The Boston Globe*, June 13, 1955, for Mackle houses in Lewis Island (adjacent to St. Petersburg in Tampa Bay) and Pompano Beach Highlands (north of Fort Lauderdale)

the largest traffic jam in Arizona history, with a hundred thousand people showing up when only ten thousand were expected.[4] As the story goes, Tom Breen, a lieutenant at Del Webb, came up with the idea to market retirement as "active retirement living" after visiting retirement communities in Arizona and Florida and witnessing residents just sitting around.[5] His forethought to build an activity-based community to sell a housing model was enormously success-ful; by the end of the millennium, the Del Webb Corporation had a portfolio of thirteen communities with more than eighty thousand homes.[6]

As land was being cleared, homes were being erected, and droves of people were moving into retirement communities across Florida and Arizona, the nascent field of gerontology was laying the theoretical foundation for, and arguing about, how people develop in older age. Two contrasting theories of note emerged that played an influential role in the cultural representation of retirement as a stage of life.[7] In 1961, in their book *Growing Old*, Elaine Cumming and William Earl Henry formulated the disen-gagement theory to describe the process of an inevitable with-drawal by older people from the rest of society. According to the theory, disengagement by older people was innate, universal, and mutual based on the deterioration of abilities resulting in a natural loss of ties to others in society. The theory postulated that societal success in an industrialized economy demands that the old retire before the inevitable deterioration of knowledge and skills that accompanies aging, thereby paving the way for the young who possesses sufficient skills to assume authority. Through the lens of disengagement theory, idle retirement was an apt life stage for people whose knowledge and skills were rapidly diminishing and who had no productive role to play.

In 1961, gerontologist Robert Havighurst pushed back and rejected the tenets of the controversial disengagement theory by proposing a counter-theory based on the maintenance of activity and social interactions in older age.[8] Activity theory posited that

Del Webb advertisement for Sun City, in *Arizona Days and Ways Magazine*, 1962.

successful aging would emerge as a positive relationship with involvement in activities that would increase life satisfaction and help older people replace lost life roles after retirement. The idea of achieving happiness and satisfaction through activity in later life was the proverbial icing on the cake for people looking to take the plunge and move into an age-restricted activity-based lifestyle community.

Taken together, the disengagement and activity theories of aging were incredibly influential toward the social construction of old age and retirement as a social institution. Whether retirees were disengaged or active, retirement was now understood as a separate stage of life during which we would be either actively entertained in hobbies or perhaps volunteer work or else acceptably withdrawn from others. The idea of older age as a time of opportunity, contribution, and meaning-making was lost. Gone were the days when older people were seen as active contributors (economically and socially) to society.

To be fair, there are incredible benefits to being retired, and many people enjoy the freedom to do what they want, when they want, without the constraints of a nine-to-five anchor or the stress of responsibilities. On the flip side, the retirement experience can be undesirable for some and not attainable for others, whether or not they would like to retire. While being forced out of a job earlier than desired, poor health, and reduced income are some of the things that can detract from happiness during retirement, a principal and unacknowledged reason for dissatisfaction is that an entire stage of life focused on leisure and activity, just for the sake of activity, is simply not enough. People of all ages need purpose, goals, and an outlet for ambitions. The freedom of time for a permanent vacation doesn't leave much space for purposeful meaning-making. After all, vacations are only special because they end.

We all need a reason to get out of bed in the morning. While different things may drive us, the need for purpose, belonging, and mattering is universal. The need for meaning-making in later life is just as great as in other stages of life, and those who are motivated by a sense of purpose are happier and live longer. In retirement, however, we lack the formal processes and outlets that enable us to pursue lives that feel purposeful and engage in activities that feel deeply meaningful. This reality is beautifully illustrated in the book *The Blue Zones*, by Dan Buettner. *The Blue Zones* project was undertaken to determine what makes the longest-lived people thrive. Five rare longevity hot spots around the globe with the highest proportion of centenarians were visited to learn about the secret recipe for a good, long life. What they found was beautiful, simple, and, quite honestly, intuitive. The lifestyle habits of the world's longest-lived people included not only healthy behaviors, like eating well and moving your body, but also psychosocial factors, like having a purpose, social networks, a sense of belonging, and being near family.[9]

One gaping hole in the abstraction of retirement as a life stage is that activity and leisure do not fill the need for a purpose-driven life. By definition, retirement is based on a deficit mind-set of *what I used to do* and *who I used to be*. To retire is to leave your job, cease to work, or withdraw from a particular place; it's more fittingly characterized as a lack-of rather than an add-on.

When introduced to new people in the United States, it is commonplace to ask straight off, "What do you do for a living?" I was shocked when I learned that this is not customary in other cultures. People in France find the question offensive and rarely consider their occupation an interesting part of their identity. When we transition to retirement, this question can be a painful reminder of *who we used to be*, especially in a culture like the one in the United States where occupational identity is so essential to how we regard ourselves. And yet, I have met countless people here in America who have introduced themselves to me by identifying as retired. That gives no information about who they are as a person other than that they used to work someplace. A status of "being retired" is devoid of identity, meaning, and roles. This is precisely why I believe that elderhood is a much more apt term for later life. By definition, *elderhood* is growth-oriented and presents the question of *who I am now* and *who I am continuing to become*. Anti-ageism through elderhood shifts our focus from who we were to who we are in the present and who we want to become in the future. Regardless of physical ability, cognitive function, socioeconomic class, level of dependency, or myriad personal identifiers, we are all still becoming. Where retirement fails to capture a universal expectation of growth and contribution, elderhood succeeds.

The retirement lifestyle sold to us as the pinnacle of our "golden years" is lacking in many ways. What about those of us who have no desire to retire? Or those who can't afford to retire? How must it feel to be constantly asked the question "Aren't you going to retire soon?" by friends, family and coworkers. I would classify this question as a classist, ageist, and ableist microaggression. This question puts someone with no intention of retiring on the defensive and forces them to explain their reasoning. Retirement as a life stage brings the expectation that the ability to move away from paid work is a normal and natural part of the life course. Underlying this expectation is the assumption that we all have the financial means to retire, a privileged perspective to say the least, and one that can be particularly offensive to those with intersectional identities that are historically oppressed or disadvantaged. Race, ethnicity, gender, social class and disability, and opportunities for educational attainment and employment create layers or levels of privilege that affect the ability to retire. Being a woman, Black, Hispanic, or disabled, for example, are all indicators that someone is more likely to experience the structural inequalities that lead to poverty. Here are a few sobering statistics:[10]

- More than twenty-five million Americans aged sixty and older are economically insecure, living at or below 250 percent of the federal poverty level.
- On average, older women receive about $4,500 less annually in Social Security benefits than men due to lower wages and caregiving responsibilities, creating lower lifetime earnings.
- The poverty rate for older people increases with age and is higher for women, blacks and Hispanics, and people in poor health.

• Older black men are twice as likely to be unemployed as older white men.

As we age, inequities accumulate and become more pronounced, a concept called cumulative disadvantage — advantages and disadvantages throughout life shape trajectories in the short and the long term.[11] Simply put, cumulative disadvantages reproduce over time, and the results of inequality are experienced exponentially in later life. Being at a disadvantage earlier in life can mean that not working in later life is simply not tenable.

Regarding retirement as a life stage also implies that the desire to stop working is an expected and normal part of later life. During the turn of the past century, when the concept of retirement emerged as a way to transition older workers out of the workforce, most jobs were physically taxing, but by the mid-twentieth century, age and ability no longer predicted work-life longevity. Therefore, assuming impending retirement based on perceived age or ability is offensive and discriminatory. Referring back to *The Blue Zones*, we are reminded that the world's longest-lived people had no doubt that a purpose-driven life was an essential ingredient to their longevity. The pursuit of a working life is one way in which people find purpose and should not be summarily dismissed because of age or ability. The social institution of retirement normalized withdrawal and disengagement for older people without providing an adequate alternative to take its place. Similarly, the proliferation of age-restricted retirement communities contributed to the erection of social and physical barriers that separated older people from the rest of society.

The New Face of Age and Ability Segregation

The homogeneity encapsulated within retirement neighborhoods acts as a collective representation of a retirement *identity* that reinforces separateness and othering. In an age-restricted community, your neighbors next door, across the street, and down the block are all similar to you. Segregation is defined as the action or state of setting something apart from others. Whether intentionally driven by policy, laws, or out of desire, the result is a separateness that blocks opportunities for people of different walks of life to meet, interact, and learn together. Frustratingly, the need and desire for age-segregated living is both a result of and an antecedent of ageism. As a result of ageism, elders feel excluded and marginalized with limited opportunities to contribute to society in a meaningful way. It is not unreasonable to think that age-based oppression would lead to the desire to physically distance from oppressors. As an antecedent of ageism, the gates, walls, and landscaping designating the perimeter of an age-restricted retirement community send a message — implicitly and explicitly — that those who live beyond the physical barriers are removed and different. This feeds the us-versus-them mentality foundational to explicit ageism. Explicit ageism occurs when we have conscious awareness and intention of thoughts, feelings, or actions toward people in other age groups; explicit ageism is deliberate and purposeful. The people on the inside of those gates become the othered out-group and the people living in our own neighborhoods the us in-group. The people who make up our personal in-group are powerful proximal influential forces that shape our identity and worldview. The people in the out-group are in the distal zone of effect with little opportunity to encourage or inspire our belief system. Consequently, age-segregated living in all forms takes age diversity out of communities and limits prospects for cross-age relationships.

Age-restricted communities also erect even more barriers to extended family living. You can't live in the same neighborhood as your intergenerational family members if your community is age-restricted. Institutionalizing retirement and formulating it as a lifestyle based on age exclusion has reinforced the vicious and complex ageism cycle. This is particularly damaging since a key mechanism to combatting fear of aging and ageism is the ability for younger and older people to spend time together organically.

Ageism is based on assumptions, judgments, and stereotypes that feed bias and discrimination, and ageism is incited when people in different age groups claim superiority over the other. Younger people sometimes feel vilified and belittled by older people, and older people sometimes feel dismissed and devalued by younger people. Age-diverse relationships nurture the respect, understanding, and learning needed to dismantle ageism. When people of different age groups live, work, play, and learn together, they develop relationships based on reciprocity. As if by magic, reciprocity bonds us together and we develop relationships as individuals rather than as stereotypes of "old" or "young." Study after study has reinforced that age-diverse relationships have physical, emotional, and psychological benefits. However, during the latter twentieth century, the trends dictated building more walls and structures to cordon off the old from the young and the abled from the disabled.

The Older Americans Act in 1965 spurred the propagation of age-restricted communities like Sun City in Arizona designed for healthy and "active" older people, and it also encouraged state and local governments to develop residential care facilities — nursing homes — to serve those with more extensive care needs. Growing out of the almshouse practices of the Industrial Revolution, residential care facilities are hospital-like in design and institutional in approach. While the lifestyle of retirement housing has been sold to older people of means, residential care facilities have targeted low-income elders and those with developmental disabilities and mental health diagnoses.[12] In the 1980s, a new subset of residential care emerged called assisted living that bridged the gap between living independently and needing skilled nursing care. Assisted living was driven by an aspiration to provide enhanced services to foster residents' well-being and preserve their self-worth in environments with homelike features.[13] It is a successful, popular model; according to the National Center for Assisted Living, there are now approximately 28,900 assisted living communities housing more than one million people in the United States.[14]

Explosive growth and expansion of the senior living industry over the past forty years has been fueled in large part by the advent of the continuing care retirement community, or CCRC, a comprehensive system of housing with varying levels of care and types of accommodations, from independent living to assisted living, skilled nursing, and memory care. In other words, CCRCs (also called life care and life plan communities) are all-inclusive long-term care organizations offering access to housing, health care, and social services on a single campus.

There are a variety of care models out there, but one crucial commonality that CCRCs spawned is yet another label to collectively describe older people — residents. In turn, the term *resident* has become an identity that reinforces separateness and othering. *Resident*, like *retiree*, is a deficient descriptor in that it fails to meaningfully describe any attributes of importance to individuality. In my opinion, using the term *resident* objectively ignores all other forms of identity and fails to acknowledge that an elder is more than a resident of their dwelling; they are individuals with purpose, goals, and contributions to make.

Although there is no dispute that the array of care options provided by the senior living industry fill critical needs and have benefited many, the fact remains that we have established and normalized the practice of warehousing older people for profit. Industry, by definition, is a group of businesses that produce particular kinds of goods or services and are typically classified based on their most significant sources of revenue. For the senior living industry, older people equal revenue. It is not my intent to dismiss or diminish the contributions of thousands of hardworking, loyal people who have dedicated themselves to providing quality care and support to those in senior living communities. I commend these assiduous individuals and have tremendous gratitude and appreciation for them. Instead, my point is that over time we have industrialized and profitized a system that was founded on the premise of age and ability exclusion; and that has contributed to ageism, ableism, and the intersection of the two.

Segregating older people is structural ageism. Segregating those with disabilities within an age-segregated community is structural ableism. And both are standard practices. Most modern long-term care communities are segregated based on level of ability — independent living, assisted living, skilled nursing, and often memory care, usually in a building or wing that is in perpetual lockdown. Those that are non-disabled typically dine separately from those who need any assistance. Activities and social events are often coordinated separately, so there is little chance for intermingling. The result is a structural system of marginalization within an already marginalized group. It is a microcosm of separateness. And this microcosm perpetuates fear of aging, fear of disability, and fear of dying.

In her book *Disrupting the Status Quo of Senior Living: A Mindshift*, Jill Vitale-Aussem describes how long-term care communities' operational and physical structures enforce segregation based on frailty and capability. She provides detailed examples of how communities not only discourage but also prohibit residents with physical and cognitive limitations from dining or participating in activities with functionally independent residents. She describes the structural hierarchy within these communities' confines that prioritizes the most active and fosters separateness of the frailest. Senior living campuses are built to separate based on ability and need by design, as this helps create efficient and effective physical environments that are safe for residents and staff members alike. It makes practical sense to have a cluster-based approach to care, but an unfortunate and unintended consequence of this design is that it fertilizes self-directed and other-directed ageism and ableism.

As a reminder, self-directed ageism describes internalized fear and discomfort associated with personal aging and being old. Have you ever heard an older person say something like, "I don't want to live/socialize/interact with all of those old people!"? "Those old people," typically peers with physical or cognitive limitations, are adjudged as others, the out-group, undesirable, frightening, and beneath. Psychologically separating yourself from others within your peer group is an outcome of fear and perceived stigma. And the physical separation maintained within senior living communities by design feeds that fear. Vitale-Aussem writes, "Where else in society would it be acceptable to segregate and marginalize people who are deemed undesirable by their peers?"[15] Just as we do, for instance in high schools to reduce the likelihood of bullying and separateness, we need mechanisms and awareness in order to avoid needless marginalization and emotional suffering.

Responding to fear of loss of ability by emotionally separating ourselves from a perceived threat is a common ego-protective behavior that shields us from anxiety. Of course, fear of loss of ability can be emotionally triggering and personally disconcerting. At the same time, it is important to acknowledge and understand how our fears of loss and dependency are societally reinforced. Growing old in a culture of manipulation requires a deeper exploration of the imperceptible forces that live beyond the edges of our consciousness. Fear of aging, disability, and dependency are by-products of the dominant cultural narrative that nurtures falsehoods. We are primed and conditioned to accept a predefined, other-defined mandate of success. Rather than looking within to create a personalized definition of success, we blindly accept societal norms that equate success with wealth, status, independence, marriage, children, career, longevity, and more. Success in aging is no different. We reclaim our personal power when we begin to see the forces that shape our understanding of success. We then have the knowledge to actively and deliberately choose a definition for ourselves.

What Is Successful Aging?

In 1987, scholars John Rowe and Robert Louis Kahn published a seminal paper titled "Human Aging: Usual and Successful" to encourage researchers to move past emphasizing age-related losses alone and broaden understanding of individual factors affecting the aging process such as diet, exercise, and personal habits.[16] This was groundbreaking work pushing back against deficiency-based schools of thought such as the biomedical model and the disengagement theory of aging. The successful aging paradigm, along with related concepts such as active aging, positive aging, healthy aging, and optimal aging, postulated that the process of aging was heterogeneous, and a framework was needed focusing on modifiable health factors to differentiate a polarity between usual and successful aging. Usual aging was determined as incorporating typical and expected losses in physiologic functions experienced with age. Successful aging was delineated as the process of aging with minimal to no physiologic loss. The intent of the successful aging paradigm was to differentiate between pathologic and nonpathologic aging — that is, older people with diseases or disabilities and those without — to spur research focused on interventions for older people without disease but at high risk due to usual intrinsic biological aging processes to develop disease. And it did indeed help to accomplish that goal. Over the next few decades, accompanying a dramatic climb in longevity, we have collectively experienced a compression of morbidity; people are living longer and healthier, with a shortened period of disease and disability closer to the end of their lives. Proactive theories like successful aging were deterministic in promoting a positive mind shift that it is never too late to develop healthy habits.

Research on the theory of successful aging undertaken between 1984 and 1993 produced a subsequent 1997 publication by Rowe and Khan titled *Successful Aging*. In this book, successful aging criteria expanded in breadth, depth, and scope to include three separate benchmarks: a low probability of disease and disease-related disability, a high cognitive and physical functional capacity, and active engagement with life.[17]

The re-envisioned concept of successful aging offered a refreshingly new perspective that dismissed the commentary that aging was solely a process of decline, thereby increasing awareness that a large portion of older people were active, healthy, and engaged members of society. The underlying conceptual framework of successful aging made clear that not all older people were frail, disengaged, and passive recipients of care. In a deliberate attempt to confront ageism, *Successful Aging* underscored that older people are vibrant, thriving, contributing, and active members of society. Astonishingly, ageism is so deeply entrenched in the public milieu that there is a broad lack of awareness of the fact that most older people remain living within their homes and communities. In myth-busting presentations on aging, I commonly ask participants to guess the percentage of older people who live in long-term care communities. The responses typically fall into the range of 50 to 70 percent, and people are generally shocked when I provide the actual statistics. In actuality, only 4.5 percent of older people live in nursing homes, and 2 percent in assisted living facilities; a whopping 93.5 majority live in the community.[18] Through the paradigm of successful aging, Rowe and Kahn were making the important point that we would be remiss, as a society, to focus on only *care of* older people and neglect emphasizing factors that contribute to the *success and thriving of* older people. Although both scholars and the public embraced this message, it came with perilous and unanticipated side effects.

Unfortunately, *successful aging* became a catchphrase that contributed to ageism and ableism, creating a chasmic view of aging as success (independence, health, ability) or failure (dependence, illness, disability). The polarity within the interpretation of successful aging was troublesome in several ways; first, it offered a narrow, limited, and often unattainable definition of success;

second, it entered hazardous territory proffering the perception of older age as reliant on the success or failure of the individual; and third, if we live long enough, it is avowedly impossible for us not to experience decline, illness, and disability. Let's dissect each issue more carefully.

A narrow, limited, and often unattainable definition of success
What is your first thought, off the top of your head, about what it means to age successfully? Does it mean that you are physically fit and bustling about at the gym while also engaged in a variety of volunteer activities? Does it mean that you are happily retired and surrounded by grandkids? Does it mean that you are simply happy to still be alive? Motivational speaker and author Zig Ziglar tells us that "true success has more components than one sentence or idea can contain."[19] According to Ziglar, success could be all of those things for one person, none of those things for another, and every combination in between.

Maintaining good health, function, and engagement with life as we age is preferable; nevertheless, it is often unachievable. To classify success at aging using any characteristic that is beyond individual control is unfair, to say the least. It inevitably places blame and shame on those who don't meet the defined criteria, which, in the case of aging, means everyone eventually. Encapsulating success using the three components of successful aging — low probability of disease and disease-related disability, high cognitive and physical functional capacity, and active engagement with life — provides an impossibly narrow path for anyone to claim their power and potential in elderhood.

As we age, we are invariably going to experience illness, decline in physical functioning, slowing in cognitive functioning, and sometimes a purposeful and deliberate retreat from engagement with others — and this is perfectly all right. Thinking back to the Botswanan concept of botsofe, it can even be argued that we need to experience physical decline to maximize our emotional and spiritual potential. Further support for a purposeful and needed downshift was also proposed in the theory of gerotranscendence by Lars Tornstam in 1994. Tornstam, a Swedish scholar, suggested that developmental aging involves a normal and natural transition in which we redefine life, death, self, and relationships, and this process often takes place in a more solitary state.[20] Simply put, the choice to retreat into a place of quiet, thoughtful reflection can be a beneficial aspect of the aging process and part of a necessary and peaceful transition toward death. For someone experiencing gerotranscendence, active engagement in the community is antithetical and disruptive to their developmental goals.

The successful aging paradigm provides a stagnant view of development by purporting that the developmental imperative of older adulthood is to maintain the status quo of midlife. Because we have collectively invested in the idea of successful aging as the continuation of activities and roles of adulthood, we have yet to define and differentiate elderhood as a separate and distinct developmental stage of life. The consequence of this mind-set is that we focus on success in older age as continued *doing* rather than *being*. Adulthood roles are intertwined with the image of productivity, and productivity is associated with value. As we transition to elderhood and naturally shift our focus to a state of being incorporating the cultivation of self and relationships, we begin to be perceived as having less productive value. Elevating the ideals of midlife roles and responsibilities as success in later life results in a shocking lack of understanding about roles, markers, and milestones specific to elderhood.

To age successfully has meant that we distance ourselves from the idea of being old or in old age, internalizing the belief that decline is a failure, stigmatizing being old, judging others with limitations, and viewing diminishment as the outcome of poorly made individual choices.

A new perception of older age as being reliant on the success or failure of the individual

In 1989, Peter Laslett wrote a controversial book titled *A Fresh Map of Life: The Emergence of the Third Age*. In it, he decreed that the "third age," defined as the culmination of one's life after retirement, was a time of great fulfillment.[21] But he provided one notable caveat — that this only applied to healthy, active elders who had a positive attitude. Furthermore, he then defined the *fourth age* as the final stage of life, characterized by decrepitude, dependence, and death. More about the fourth age a little later; for now, let's take a closer look at how the concept of the third age evolved alongside successful aging to create a seismic ripple in the public's view of aging.

Two diametrically opposing representations of being old emerged, reflecting the sentiments of the third age and successful aging. On the one hand, we have the older person that goes skydiving at eighty-two, climbs a mountain at eighty-seven, writes their first novel at ninety-one, and wins the Nobel Peace Prize at ninety-four — the epitome of success in later life. On the other hand, we see an older person with cognitive challenges, or in a wheelchair, or living with physical frailty, or living in isolation as the personification of failure in later life. Taking one more step toward the edge of a perilous cliff, we assign individual blame for these conditions. Successful super-agers took care of themselves by eating right, exercising, saving money, and working hard. Other people have no one to blame but themselves as they failed to heed the sound advice given over the years. Yes, I am being dramatic and somewhat hyperbolic to illustrate a point. We have a broadly accepted notion that successful aging is the responsibility of the individual. Not only is this ridiculously untrue, but it also ignores outright classist, structural, and political forces that shape the aging experience.

Biological aging is the result of genetics, environment, and individual lifestyle characteristics. Research demonstrates that approximately 25 percent of the variation in longevity is due to genetics, while environmental and lifestyle factors account for most.[22] That said, we don't age in isolated bubbles where genes, environment, and phenotypic characteristics separately determine the outcomes of health and longevity. Remember the nature-versus-nurture debate we learned in grade school? There is no debate; aging and development are transactional and influenced by genotype, phenotype, and environment. Furthermore, we must also consider that environmental factors can affect genetic expression, a concept called epigenetics. Epigenetic changes are driven by external or internal influences — stress, poverty, pollution, trauma — that change our genes' expression.

Recognizing the impact of epigenetics, it is blindingly unreasonable to place the onus of successful aging on the individual. Revisiting the concept of cumulative disadvantage, it is undeniable that intersectional levels of discrimination and structural disadvantages negatively affect aging. As a result, health disparities are indissolubly linked to race, ethnicity, gender, sexual orientation, and socioeconomic position. Here are just a few statistics representative of the impact of social and environmental influences on health and longevity:

- People who have attained the highest educational levels can expect to live an average of six years longer than those who only attained the lowest levels.[23]
- Socioeconomic position can account for 80 percent of the life expectancy divide between black and white men and 70 percent between black and white women.[24]
- Cancer mortality was 15 percent higher and cardiovascular disease mortality was 28 percent higher for blacks than for whites.[25]
- A higher incidence of victimization experienced by lesbian, gay, and bisexual older adults is associated with poorer general health, more depressive symptoms, and more significant disability.[26]

When we focus blame for not aging optimally on the individual, we are summarily dismissing the contributions of the institutions and political structures that have contributed toward inequity. Not only is placing responsibility to age well entirely on the individual lazy, privileged, and unethical thinking, doing so serves to widen longevity disparities and systemic inequity in elderhood.

The impossibility of not experiencing decline, illness, and disability
I was recently waiting in line to purchase groceries at the store and noticed a picture of actress Betty White on a tabloid with the headline GIVING UP ON LIFE AT 98. It was a powerful reminder that we see death as a failure despite the fact that the process of aging will invariably lead to decline and eventually to death. This is the nature of mortality. At the end of the day, we can give in to the negative messages and try with all of our might to fight the inevitable or empower ourselves to accept, and even embrace, the process of aging and dying.

The definition of successful aging as the maintenance of health, function, and engagement eventually eliminates everyone from claiming success. It sets up a straw man fallacy that keeps us from facing our deep-rooted fears of dependence, loss, and death. The differentiation of the third age from the fourth age was an attempt to make this truism more palatable. Instead, it delays the inevitable realization that we will all experience illness, decline, and disability. It also distances us from tapping in to our capacity to accept, adapt, create meaning, and grow alongside diminishment. *The diminishment is not the failure; the inability to accept it is.*

There is a video produced by AARP called *Millennials Show Us What "Old" Looks Like* that asks selected millennials aged nineteen through thirty-three to describe what an old person looks like and what age they consider to be old.[27] They are then promptly introduced to a real "old" person (aged fifty-five through seventy-five). The two people spend a few minutes together teaching each other a physical activity (yoga, karate, dancing). At the end of this quality time, the millennials are asked once more what age they consider to be old. In the course of just a few short minutes, the millennials back away from their initial claims of forty to fifty and offer a more socially acceptable range of eighty to a hundred, or later. The exercise claims to challenge outdated beliefs about aging and ageism. Does it, though? I sure don't think so.

The exercise does not fundamentally alter or challenge ageist stereotypes but rather pushes the stigma further down the road. Shifting old from forty or fifty to eighty or ninety does not change the fact that *old* is still being blatantly stigmatized. The exercise also reinforces the idea of successful aging as physical activity and independence, raising our anxiety and discomfort with aging and the inevitability of decline and death. Compounding matters, the AARP video also stereotypes Millennials as clueless and immature. Rather than diminishing our fears, it provides fertile soil for cultivating ageism. Ageism will not cease without the acknowledgment that with aging we become old. I have experienced tremendous frustration with countless well-intended anti-ageism attempts that have demonized being old. It represents a fundamental flaw in many current interventions and strategies. We have socially constructed old to be a pejorative, and the time has come for it to be reclaimed. The illusion created by the differentiation of the third from the fourth age has further inflamed and stoked fears of aging, oldness, dependency, and death.

Terror management theory proposes that a psychological conflict arises from the dissonance between our innate instinct for self-preservation and the realization that death is inevitable.[28] Concerning ageism, old people represent a threat to young people by reminding them of their own fate — loss of health, beauty, function, status, and, ultimately, death. It is not surprising to think that we want to push away people who trigger our existential fears. It is far easier to label, categorize, classify, and ultimately reject those we deem as frightening from our physical and emotional spaces. Exercises like the AARP video that enhance the distinction between old as active (third age) versus old as frail (fourth age) perpetuate existential fears of our future selves. The desire to psychologically protect ourselves by blocking out the perceived threats associated with aging leads to internalized oppression. Internalized oppression is fostered by the social cultural ideals providing the narrative of the final stage of life as a state of decrepitude and dependence. The result is that we disassociate ourselves from identifying as aging.

I Am Not Old — Internalized Oppression

I remember the first time that someone called me old. I was at a party with a friend of mine who was a good fifteen years younger than I. Someone jokingly referred to me as old and asked if I was her mother. I felt sharp stabs as if I had been injured and heat rising up my body to my reddening face. I was mortified. At the time, I didn't have the cognizance to parse why I felt so insulted nor the skills to craft a coherent response. I just felt small. It took years for me to unpack that experience and identify that the comment had made me feel irrelevant, unattractive, and unimportant. That is some heavy emotion for being called a three-letter word. *Old* packs a punch.

Why do you think the word *old* is so stigmatized? Think for a moment about what images it brings to mind. Perhaps a frail person. What thoughts and feelings emerge? Perhaps someone irrelevant. Now, notice how value-laden these impressions are. We typically don't value frail or irrelevant people.

Years later, I finally understood that *old* was not inherently good or bad but rather a signifier of being long-lived. I also noticed the great lengths we will go to protect and shield ourselves from being identified as or called out as old. We do blatant things like dyeing our hair, wearing makeup to cover wrinkles, or even undergoing cosmetic surgery. We also do less obvious things to deflect, such as say, "I am not old; I am just mature!" In this comment, we see a denial and dissociation with being old and attempting to cover up this shame and embarrassment with a more palatable and acceptable Band-Aid description. Euphemisms for *old*, like *mature*, *seasoned*, *vintage*, and *experienced*, are used in attempts to conceal the stigmatizing wound inflicted by the use of *old*.

Have you ever heard someone older say something like, "There is still so much to learn even at my age!" At first blush, that statement seems benign, but take a closer look. *Still* and *even* are little words that are immensely significant. In this context, these words imbue a sentiment of surprise that someone has the capacity and interest to learn in older age. It is subtle, which makes it so dangerous, and it is pernicious. Ageist remarks can also be disguised as compliments, such as calling an older person a young lady or young man. The intent behind describing an older person as young is to boost self-image or infer that someone is energetic, lively, or active. In reality, this is not a compliment but rather a subtle perpetuation of the idea that old is something to be avoided.

We communicate about aging with others, reinforcing our sense of self and the self-image that drives all aspects of our identity. As with gender, race, and ability, age identity is created, reinforced, and sustained through normed practices and a collective societal understanding. Age is one of the more fluid forms of identity in that we continually form and re-form how we experience the world as we age. Age dictates whether we can go to school, get a driver's license, and collect Social Security benefits. We feel differently about ourselves and interact differently with the world at age twenty than we do at forty, sixty, or eighty. Yet we don't often take the time to critically evaluate, explore, and reflect on our own aging identity. Most of us learn about aging through personal relationships, if we are fortunate enough to have a relationship with an older person, or from the culture at large. The larger culture is riddled with language, images, songs, cards, and messages devaluing aging. Collectively these cultural artifacts reinforce the social construction of age. Discrimination, oppression, and marginalization result from these social constructions that generally place value on youth over the aged.

Ability is another form of identity that changes over time. We can experience changes to ability at any time and often do at multiple points during our lifetime. As with age identity, we are faced with creating and re-creating our identity in relation to our level of abilities. Think about a time you or a loved one experienced an illness or injury and required crutches, a cane, a wheelchair, or a walker. Traversing the world becomes quite different and often an unexpected challenge. You notice that doorways aren't as wide as you thought, bathrooms are difficult to navigate, and the world seems to be moving very quickly. It is easy to notice others' frustration trying to walk around you or past you to get where they need to go. If you have ever experienced this, you have caught a glimpse of ableism at personal, relational, and structural levels.

CHAPTER FIVE

The Era of Manipulation: Anti-Aging Culture

My face carries all my memories. Why would I erase them?

— Diane von Furstenberg

When I was a teenager, my brother Jeff and I decided to try an experiment using our dad as the subject. We had a running joke in the family that Dad had a shocking level of unawareness about his susceptibility to food cravings, such as seeing an ad and feeling like he had to get himself some of that immediately. One day, Jeff and I decided to test his level of susceptibility by periodically but consistently mentioning pizza as the day progressed. We would sing songs under our breath about pizza, casually mention ingredients in pizza, and bring up words like *pie* or *slice* as often as we could. We thought for certain that Dad would catch on before the end of the day. He didn't. When it was time to talk about the dinner plan for the evening, as if on cue, Dad said, "I'm not sure why but I have been in the mood for pizza all day!" My dad may have been more vulnerable than most, especially when it came to food, but we are all susceptible to this type of manipulation.

As we go about our days with never-ending to-do lists demanding our time and attention, insidious and powerful subliminal messaging worms its way into our thoughts. The constant barrage of voices and images in the background seeps into our subconscious with little notice. The media is a potent force of manipulation, frequently playing on our fears because that approach most often translates into ratings or sales. Decades of research show that fear-based advertising is incredibly effective, largely because fear is contagious.[1]

From the time I was a little girl, I remember thinking that Nonny was beautiful. I particularly loved her strikingly gorgeous silver hair and the soft crêpey skin on her face and hands. Nonny had friends who underwent plastic surgery to tighten their sagging under-eye, neck, or chin areas, and when one of them encouraged her to do the same, she dismissed the idea with, "Why? I'm not eighteen." Having Nonny as a role model provided some armor with which to shield myself from the barrage of age-related appearance fear and shaming that I would encounter, directly and indirectly, over the ensuing years. I have witnessed friends and acquaintances become addicted to plastic surgery once gravity took over. It might start with a peel and then expand to fillers, a face-lift, Botox, and CoolSculpting, all in an effort to "look younger." I have overheard conversations among people still in their twenties discussing the right age to schedule that first derma-tologist appointment to establish an anti-aging skin care plan.

I am not opposed to products or procedures that make people feel good about themselves. Beauty is personal and subjective, and everyone should be free to do as they please. By all means, dye your hair, get the procedure, purchase the cream, and put on the cosmet-ics. My concern has to do with the underlying feelings that drive these behaviors — namely, fear and shame. There is an important distinction between desire and shame, and the anti-aging industry capitalizes on the latter. Underneath this shame lies a vision of what it means to be old, along with a fear driven by (mis)under-standing of the importance of elders in society.

Anti-aging agents reinforce the successful aging paradigm, the idea that looking and acting like those who are middle-aged or younger should be a primary objective as we grow older. The unspoken effect of this outlook is the promulgation of the idea that "aging well" is the responsibility of and under the control of the individual. Those who show the physical signs of advanced age are judged and blamed for their own failure. In this manner, the anti-aging industry has fabricated yet another obstacle to developing an appreciation and understanding of the unique gifts and opportunities inherent in elderhood. To fully appreciate the profound impact of the anti-aging movement, it's necessary to understand the power structures and dynamics that create the social construction of old age. Who profits from ageism?

The quest to deter wrinkles and maintain soft and supple skin is nothing new, but the widely accepted term *anti-aging* is relatively recent. You can go as far back as 69 BCE in ancient Egypt and learn that Cleopatra took daily baths in donkey milk to preserve her skin's beauty and vitality and reduce wrinkles. In the Elizabethan era in the 1500s, women placed raw meat on their faces; in the 1700s, aged wine as a skin care regimen was in favor. What existed in the past as a casual practice has become a thriving and profitable consumer industry. As of 2020, the global market for anti-aging products is estimated at $52.5 billion a year and is projected to reach $83.2 billion by 2027.[2] Companies are making *a lot* of money profiting from ageism. Women have been the primary target, but men are not impervious to fear-based ageist marketing and are increasingly pitched youth-oriented skin care products and shame-based virility supplements and "cures."

The institutions and entities that profit from anti-aging play a pivotal role in establishing standards for beauty and success as well as gender ideals of femininity and masculinity. Anti-aging rhetoric is eschewed and appeals are subtle, silently feeding our insecurities, driving our consumption of products through fear and shame and promoting other-directed and self-directed ageism.

The Anti-Aging Movement

The anti-aging industry encompasses both anti-aging medicine and anti-aging commercial products. Taken as a whole, the anti-aging movement is dedicated to eliminating or reversing the appearance and effects of aging.

Exercising control over biological aging has been an ambition throughout time; think of Ponce de León searching for the fountain of youth in the 1500s. But it was during the early 1900s, as the almshouses were transitioning to modern-day nursing homes, that old age came to be considered a decrepit, disease-laden existence that imposed a burden on society. This perception served as a catalyst for medical research to try to develop an actual cure for aging, some intervention that would help stop the vicissitudes of the aging process that result in older people requiring so much time and support from younger people. Although efforts were made in the first half of the twentieth century, nothing came close to delivering miracle treatments. A formalized subdiscipline of gerontology, biogerontology, was established in the latter twentieth century, focusing on mechanisms to understand and intervene in the processes of biological aging. The emergence of biogerontology led to the establishment of the American Academy of Anti-Aging Medicine (A4M) in 1993, which in turn led to a forceful renewal of efforts to confront aging as a treatable disease. I say "forceful" with intent and purpose; A4M used militaristic terminology to describe the *fight* or *battle* to end aging. Around the same time, the view of aging as a disease to be treated and conquered was further supported by the World Health Organization, which in 1992 established aging as a disease classification (called senility) in the tenth version of the International Classification of Diseases (ICD). Furthermore, an updated extension code for old age was approved and implemented in the ICD-11 in 2019. Old age was officially labeled a disease.

It is undeniable that research in biogerontology and life extension medicine have made groundbreaking advances in detecting, treating, and preventing disease associated with aging that has vastly improved quality of life, health span, and longevity. Simultaneously, it is irrefutable that the anti-aging movement has profoundly influenced the social structures that support ageist thought and practice.

Social structures are influenced by language, language reflects the social systems, and social systems are drivers of power dynamics. Language is a powerful tool used to manipulate and persuade, and it is a strong influencer of social norms. Language about aging that expresses value perpetuates and normalizes ageism. Using the term *anti-aging* is deeply problematic in itself. The nomenclature reinforces a singular view of aging as decline and disease and strips us of the power to understand and promote aging as a state of growth and development. *Anti-aging* literally means to be against aging. If aging is the universal lifelong biological, psychological, social, and spiritual process of developing over time, how can anyone support the antithesis to this? It is a lazy and irresponsible way to describe the intended goal of increasing health span, longevity, and vitality. It could easily be referred to instead as pro-longevity or anti-senescence, promoting a clearer delineation between the detrimental effects of biological aging and *aging*. The term *anti-aging* is dangerous because it demeans and marginalizes the very process of living — which is aging.

In the 1980s, the cosmetics industry adopted the anti-aging vernacular and went all-in on the combative language used by anti-aging medicine to *fight*, *battle*, and *win the war against* the visible signs of aging. The ageist ideology of the biomedicalization of skin, which is the most visible marker of aging, was widely adopted by the mass media, and the anti-aging industry thrived as a result. The strategy was brilliant. What could be more profitable than establishing demand for a product that will never meet its intended goal? The quest to be wrinkle-free and to reject the visible signs of aging takes us down yet another path to nowhere. Again, we are giving power to others, outsiders, strangers, to define our own story of success.

Wrinkles are, literally and figuratively, frowned upon because someone else said so. This doesn't have to be the case. There are examples in nature of things that we deem more beautiful because of their age, like a tree. I happen to be obsessed with trees. I see a form of beauty in a tree that routinely changes moods, shapes, layers, and colors while simultaneously maintaining its deeply rooted sense of self. I am drawn to older trees with their thick trunks, intricate bark, and towering limbs. To me, an old tree is far more complex and magnificent than a sapling. We can apply this appreciation to older faces if we so choose.

Another manipulative expression weaponized by anti-aging industry, and sadly also by some anti-ageist initiatives, is "to be ageless," something that is both impossible and unwise. Betty Friedan wrote:

> How long, and how well, can we really live by trying to pass as young? By the fourth face-lift (or third?) we begin to look grotesque, no longer human. [We are] obsessed with stopping age, passing as young . . . seeing age only as decline from youth, we make age itself the problem — and never face the real problems that keep us from evolving and leading continually useful, vital, and productive lives. Accepting that dire mystique of age for others, even as we deny it for ourselves, we ultimately create or reinforce the conditions of our own dependence, powerlessness, isolation, even senility.[3]

The surreptitious manipulation ingrained in the anti-aging mystique promotes an environment in which we marginalize old people at our own expense by creating a hostile environment for our future selves. As Todd Nelson said, ageism is prejudice against our feared future self.[4]

Age is a unique form of self-identity in that it is ever-changing. Given that we can't know what it is like to be older than we are, we use popular culture as a guidepost to measure expectations and standards of success. This is what makes anti-aging advertising so powerful and dangerous.

Ageism embedded within the anti-aging industry marginalizes people in gendered ways as well. Gendered ageism represents the intersection of age and gender identity that leads to increased vulnerability. The ideals of femininity and masculinity are rooted in the social construct of gender and are expressed as gender roles and traits. Masculine/feminine appeal is an advertising strategy that marketing professionals have adopted to influence purchasing behavior.[5] The following discussion provides references to cisgender (and stereotypical) women and men; however, the ideology of femininity and masculinity is intended to represent the continuum of gender identity.

Femininity and Anti-Aging

Anti-aging remedies targeted at women to improve wrinkles, mask gray hair, and soften skin have existed for millennia. However, the modern-day anti-aging industry began in earnest as early as the nineteenth century. Magazine advertisements used guilt and insecurity to help sell products that promised to give "the flesh the resiliency and freshness of youth," encouraged the virtues of "a young face at any age," and promoted the ideal of "looking 20 years younger"[6] The anti-aging industry has construed the older woman as a person at risk who must treat and prevent any markers of old age in order to not be a victim.

Femininity is susceptible to multiple marginalizations, including ageism, sexism, lookism (appearance), sizeism, fitnessism, healthism, and sexual objectification. Ironically, the vulnerability that older women face due to these layered forms of prejudice translates into being simultaneously hyper-visible and invisible. Hyper-visibility results from the exaggerated focus on appearance promoted and enabled in media by the anti-aging industry and those who have been influenced by it. It is also fostered by the rhetoric of successful aging, which posits that aging successfully essentially translates into *not* aging, and that objectively looking younger provides a shield against appearance-based age shaming.

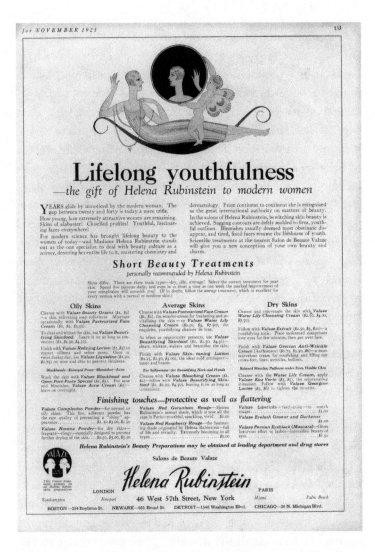

For example, telling someone "You look old" is considered an insult and is tied to implications of ugliness, failure, and inadequacy. Invisibility is a counter-effect of ageism, especially in the workplace, where older women often find their contributions dismissed or ignored and are objectively less likely to get hired or promoted.

The intersection of ageism and sexism is not limited to appearance, and there are many profound consequences to the disadvantaged position of older women. Briefly, some contributing factors of intersectional discrimination are lifelong pay differences contributing to increased poverty, increased risk of abuse and violence in later life, loss of relationships/life partners, and workplace harassment and discrimination. These are exacerbated further for women of color who are oppressed because of their racial identity and a lifetime of structural forces that contribute to inequality in later life. The effects of ageism, racism, and sexism combined exponentially increase the risk for housing instability, food insecurity, and lack of access to health care. There is, however, one silver lining for older women of color; as explained by Afiya Mbilshaka: Black women are less likely to use anti-aging products due to a stronger, more positive relationship with elderhood in a subculture where looking older is indicative of status and power.[7]

Masculinity and Anti-Aging

The anti-aging industry has benefited from equating masculinity with virility and successful aging with maintaining virility while growing older. In her publication "Firming the Floppy Penis," Toni Callasanti describes the dual images of manhood as "playing hard" and "staying hard" and explores the challenges of achieving these ideals in older age.[8] Playing hard emphasizes an achievement-oriented consumeristic model of success built upon the continuation of midlife activities and roles. Playing hard feeds right into the masculine traits of wealth, strength, and success and represents the epitome of the leisure-based active-living retirement dream sold by Sun City. Staying hard embodies masculinity in older age as continued sexual functionality and potency. You don't need to look far to find ads for low-T (testosterone) and erectile dysfunction elixirs, libido support, and stamina and sexual enhancement products. Look no further than Viagra, Pfizer's renowned erectile dysfunction drug, which banked $500 million in revenue in 2019 alone.[9]

Appearance-based shaming is also used on men. The men's skin care industry reached $10 billion in 2019 thanks to an ever-increasing demand for anti-aging products.[10] The ideal of masculinity as superior physical strength is just as salient in older age as it is for younger men. Older men with muscular physiques and impressive physical fitness are idolized in the media, making the loss of ability with age for men that much more stigmatized. Masculinity dictates that men are providers, and loss of provider status due to retirement, illness, or lack of ability can be a detriment to self-esteem and self-image. Societally we have yet to define elderhood in a meaningful way that redefines masculinity by acknowledging new roles and contributions for men in later life.

With an undue focus on maintaining physical and emotional strength, the normal and expected losses in physical health and stamina that come with aging can provoke deep-seated fears of dependence and burden within men. As we grow older, we will inevitably require care and also often find ourselves in relationships in which we are care providers. So-called toxic masculinity, a societal norm that equates emotionlessness and even aggression with manhood, can derail opportunities for caring and showing vulnerability when they conflict with the ideal of rugged independence. In truth, however, husbands are widely responsible for providing care to their partners, and research has demonstrated that despite notions of what it means to be an old man in a "woman's domain," men often find caregiving to be an important and significant role that can provide worth and, paradoxically, can reaffirm their sense of masculinity.[11]

The disassociation of masculinity and care-providing roles has been perpetuated (and exaggerated) since the 1950s. For example, the concept and term *stay-at-home dad* didn't become commonplace until the 2000s, and it is still not fully embraced without stigma.[12] Not long ago, as I was window-shopping one day, I noticed a baby's onesie that had "directions for Dad" printed on the garment itself so that a man would know how to put it on and snap it up. It was a not-so-gentle reminder that men are seen as bumbling and helpless caregivers. It wasn't long ago that dads were asked to "babysit" for their own children while their wives ran an errand. Similarly, anti-aging discourse reinforces gender ideology, shaping values, attitudes, and beliefs about appropriate gender roles and the constitution of femininity and masculinity.

The anti-aging industry's power is indissociably linked with visual depictions of older people in the media. We strive to emulate the models, celebrities, and fitness gurus who are touted in the media as optimally aging. Together the anti-aging movement and visual media have created the single most powerful platform to shape widely held beliefs about aging. The anti-aging movement encompassing anti-aging medicine, cosmetics, and pharmaceuticals has been incredibly influential in putting a face to the image of successful aging, both literally and figuratively.

Visual ageism describes the visual underrepresentation and/or misrepresentation of older people in the media.[13] Visual media is everywhere in our daily lives, and the images we see influence perceptions of self and others. Two separate and distinct narratives of older people are commonly portrayed in the media: the stereotypical "super-ager" who is active, energetic, and defying age-based typecasts — such as a weight lifter or marathon runner — and the stereotypical silly, senile, or frail older person. This dichotomy offers limited understanding or appreciation of the nuances, depth, and complexity of what it means to be older and creates a paucity of realistic role models in older age.

Allure magazine was the first popular publication to take a stand against anti-aging in its September 2017 issue. Actress Helen Mirren was featured on the cover with the proudly displayed headline THE END OF ANTI-AGING: OUR CALL TO THE INDUSTRY. I commend *Allure* for recognizing their contribution to ageism and taking responsible action to change the narrative. Unfortunately, in reality, *Allure* did not eliminate anti-aging mentality but simply rebranded and repackaged it. First, the beautiful Helen Mirren was clearly wearing a mask of makeup hiding her naturally aging skin in a touched-up photograph, and second, the issue was filled with products that were, well, anti-aging in intent. *Allure* took a stand again in their November 2019 issue featuring actress Sharon Stone on the cover with the same THE END OF ANTI-AGING headline, and yet again the turn of a page revealed a full-page advertisement informing me of how to best "visibly plump skin and reduce wrinkles." To add to my confusion, the cover featuring a very blond Sharon Stone also promoted a story inside on "The Glory of Going Gray."

Advocating for being anti-anti-aging is an excellent start, but to make any meaningful strides, such a gesture must be accompanied by complementary, not contradictory, images and content. Following up that statement — *I am anti-anti-aging!* — with ads selling anti-wrinkle cream is the definition of dissonance, confusing at best and damaging at worst. The easiest path to resolve this dissonance and discomfort is to advance a belief system that supports a desire for younger-looking appearance as not inherently ageist. Only it is. And as we know, the more we internalize and self-direct ageist attitudes, the more we are at risk for decreasing our own well-being and happiness.

Visual Ageism and Media

The media reflects and often directs societal norms and practices. Representation of older people in media provides context and cues that influence our valuation of aging. In general, older people have been underrepresented in the media; when elders are included, they are commonly portrayed in unrealistic ways that are exaggerated or distorted and overly homogenized.[14]

Children are often first exposed to images of aging through literature and picture books. Some of the earliest fairy tales and classic stories we hear as children depict aging as a sad and sick time of life. Characters like the wicked old witch and the beautiful young princess set the stage for binary value-based thinking of old as bad and young as good. Older people are represented as characters like doddering fools, spinsters, hags, and people yearning for the beauty and vitality that was stripped away by the ravages of time. Consider for a moment classic tales like Little Red Riding Hood, Snow White, and Hansel and Gretel. To top it off, early children's literature is a double whammy of ageism and sexism, with women particularly vulnerable to stereotyping as evil spinsters. Classic children's cartoons and movies do not fare much better with characters like Cruella de Vil from 101 *Dalmatians* and Ursula in *The Little Mermaid*.

Shows for older children and tweens can be equally guilty of devaluing older people. I have memories of watching networks like Nickelodeon and Disney XD with my children and hearing comments embedded in shows about a grandmother who "lost her mind" as well as an episode of a popular tween show in which the main characters pretended to be old people by walking with canes and yelling at each other in a demeaning tone as if they were deaf. Through the images, pictures, and stories reflected in the visual media, children become exposed to social values and learn about what it means to be old.

Children internalize negative stereotypes well before they can understand their relevance. This means that we develop fears of getting old and can start to dislike and distrust older people from a very young age. Ageism is not innate; it is learned. Because children learn through role modeling, it is even more impactful that we — their older parents, grandparents, and schoolteachers — are the very people exposing them through bedtime stories and movie nights. To be fair, people can't change what they don't see, and this type of relational ageism is not something that is widely seen or understood. Now that we know better, we can do better. You can find information on excellent book choices with positive and meaningful portrayals of older adults by visiting a website developed by Sandra McGuire, a nurse, educator, and advocate for combating ageism. You can find it by typing "Dr. Sandra McGuire booklist" into any search engine or going directly to the link: https://library .Imunet.edu/booklist.

Before we move on from the topic of visual ageism directed at children, I must seize the opportunity to mention a common ageist custom that drives me absolutely crazy, and which I mentioned briefly in the preface to this book. In classrooms across the Unted States, it is not uncommon for young children to celebrate their one hundredth day of school by dressing up as a one-hundred-year-old. Every year I see pictures posted on social media accounts, adorned with "like" and "love" icons, of children dressed in frumpy clothing, using walkers, with curlers in their hair and wearing glasses. I would like to state for the record that this is not cute, not funny, and not advisable. The exercise is demeaning; it creates caricatures of older people and feeds pervasive assumptions, judgments, and prejudices about being old. Thankfully, we (generally) no longer accept oppressive forms of cultural appropriation and we don't support insensitive impersonations of others, with one glaring exception: old people. Why not celebrate the hundredth day of school in ways that don't demoralize an entire population? Count a hundred jelly beans or make a picture out of a hundred Cheerios. Better yet, have children talk about who they hope to be when they are one hundred or what a one-hundred-year-old has contributed to the world. Why not take the opportunity to start teaching our children about aging and give them a head start toward creating their own meaningful version of elderhood? Rant complete.

Television took the mantle as the nation's most vivid and prolific learning environment in the 1950s. Television viewing increased exponentially throughout the twentieth century and into the first decade of the twenty-first, although we now refer to TV programs, commercials, movies, print advertisements, photography, and other imagery collectively as visual media.

The sphere of influence that visual media wields regarding attitudes toward old age and older people cannot be overstated. From

the 1980s to the 2000s, television reigned supreme. With the proliferation of cable systems, the recurrent images and messages
emanating from our TV screens were virtually inescapable. Prime-
time network shows captured millions of viewers seeking enter-
tainment in situation comedies, dramas, magazine-format
programs, and reality shows. Although older people made up
almost 13 percent of prime-time viewership in the 1990s, only 3
percent of characters, both male and female, and in major and
supporting roles, were sixty-five or older.[15]

Not surprisingly, gender and racial representations were also
skewed. Women and people of color were overwhelmingly underrepresented, and older women were generally portrayed as significantly younger than their male counterparts.[16] One contributing
factor was that, in the 1990s, the majority of writing jobs for both
television and film were occupied by white men under forty.[17]
There has been some progress in the decades that have followed
— in 2014, the average age of a screenwriter on a top-grossing film
was just under forty-seven, and the average age of a Hollywood
director just under fifty[18] — but clearly, there is still room for
increased diversity.

Underrepresentation wasn't the only problem regarding the
portrayal of elders. Older people that enjoyed any meaningful
screen time were commonly depicted as caricatures through tropes
like the wise but ridiculous old person, the silly demented old
person, the dirty old man, the evil old witchlike woman, the stodgy
grandmother, or the frail old person needing help crossing the
street. Exceptions like *The Golden Girls* and *Murder She Wrote* were
notable rays of sunshine, but then again, they fell into the trap of
an overly optimistic portrayal of older people as healthy and
wealthy. An exaggerated sense of prosperity perpetuates the dissonance between the idealized view of successful aging and the
actual realities of aging. Speaking of *Murder She Wrote*, this highly
successful show that ran for ten years was canceled at the height of
its popularity. Despite the show's ratings and the enormous

purchasing power of older people, the primary viewing audience was considered too old and not profitable enough for advertisers. I have to wonder if this results from trying to sell older people things we think they need — reading glasses and fall alert systems — rather than things that they actually *want*.

Television and advertising go hand in hand; programming is literally determined by profitability from advertising. Advertising brandishes a tremendously powerful influence on societal ideals, values, and mainstream culture. I would bet that, like me, you could conjure up the melody and lyrics to commercials from your youth within a second or two. In the 1970s, Americans were exposed to approximately five hundred to sixteen hundred ads per day from a variety of sources including billboards, newspapers and magazines, radio, and of course TV.[19] By 2007 that number had jumped to five thousand ads per day due to online and digital marketing. The average person in 2020 is estimated to encounter between six and ten thousand ads every single day.[20] Advertising is super-duper potent stuff.

In the 1950s and 1960s, the advertising industry homed in on the eighteen-to-forty-nine age group as primary targets for advertising. Targeting younger consumers is a commonplace tactic because younger people are known to be active consumers and influential in the purchasing decisions of friends and family. Advertisements routinely feature younger people as a catchall to appeal to and reach all consumers. It is likely that older viewers will find younger people visually appealing but not vice versa. Why? Ageism. Older people demonstrate a greater affinity for advertisements featuring younger people because ageism causes older people to disassociate with their own aging and connect with popular and acceptable notions of youth and beauty. This dynamic becomes particularly salient when the majority of advertisements that do feature older people are horrifically ageist and demeaning. Here are just a few examples of blatantly ageist commercials in the past few decades:

- A grandfather's hand is shaking so much that his grandson makes a joke out of it by capitalizing on his condition and having him shake up a soft drink bottle. (This example's blatant ageism isn't even the most offensive thing about it; the subtle age bias that infiltrates our psyche to silently shape our attitudes about aging is what's really scary.)
- A car commercial features a famous rock star de-aging as he drives a race car in reverse. At the end of the race, he emerges to a swath of fans with the headline FEEL SOMETHING AGAIN — POWERED BY YOUTH.
- A fast-food commercial features older people in a nursing home who escape one evening to stay up all hours of the night pulling pranks, dancing in clubs, and being reckless to the headline VIVA YOUNG.

Whether or not we consciously allow it, marketing and advertising have a substantive influence on developing and maintaining fears of aging and discrimination toward older people. Despite your best efforts to tune it out by turning away, there is a *Clockwork Orange* effect where it is impossible to close your eyes completely. We can't help but allow the messaging from advertising to seep into our unconscious. Undoubtedly and invariably, people will push back against my disdain for ageist advertising with the claim, "But it's funny!" It might make you smile or laugh, but if it demonizes, demoralizes, or dehumanizes, it should be reconsidered. As I previously suggested, you can put an ad to the test by considering how it would hold up if you substituted another identity characteristic — race, gender, ethnicity — for the older person, and behavior that plays on a stereotype for that group. I predict that you would no longer find it funny.

Advertising has a profound effect on how people understand life, values, and behaviors, and there exists a moral imperative for advertising to promote respect and worth for people of all ages. If social justice and ethics aren't reason enough, there are also plenty of opportunities to profit. *Longevity economy* is a term that represents all the economic activity driven by the needs of Americans aged fifty and older, including the products and services they purchase and the economic activity their spending generates.[21] And it is substantial. In 2015, there were more than 1.6 billion people in the world fifty and older. That is a significant number of older consumers contributing to economic growth and value. A shift is under way, and the advertising and marketing industries have an unprecedented opportunity to recognize the incredible economic potential of elderhood and to capitalize on it while at the same time contributing to improved societal attitudes about aging.

The Aged as Consumers

In the second half of the twentieth century, the glamorization of retirement provided a new vision of aging that differentiated healthy older age (the third age) from the diseases of older age (the fourth age). Images of active, healthy, independent older people with plenty of disposable income filled magazine, newspaper, and TV advertisements. The ascent of the anti-aging movement in the 1990s was accompanied by a deliberate push within the marketing industry to capitalize on older people as consumers. Books began to flood the market with titles such as *The 55+ Market: Exploring a Golden Opportunity* and *Marketing to Older Consumers: A Handbook of Information Strategy*. Attempts to place older people into categories such as the young-old (fifty-five to seventy-five), the old-old (seventy-five-plus), and the oldest-old (eighty-five-plus) accompanied the growing effort to understand and develop a new agenda of aging that would best appeal to older consumers.

In his 1996 book *Gerontographics: Life-Stage Segmentation for Marketing Strategy Development*, George Moschis discussed the benefits of taking a market segmentation approach to reach older adult consumers. Moschis posited that a shotgun approach to marketing to a large demographic was not efficacious because of differences in attitudes, values, and purchasing behaviors within subgroups of older adults. Targeted marketing based on segmentation analysis would be a much more effective strategic approach to what he called the mature market. To his credit, Moschis recognized and integrated the complexities and richness of the aging experience into his segmentation model. Rather than propose subgroups based on age alone, he took a comprehensive tack that accounted for psychological and lifestyle factors. His progressive approach recognized the individual and multidimensional nature of aging, and his model identified and named four gerontographic segments: Healthy Hermits, Healthy Indulgers, Ailing Outgoers, and Frail Recluses.[22] Healthy Hermits were in good health although psychologically withdrawn from society with little interest in staying active, while Healthy Indulgers were in good health, independent, and active, with disposable income. Ailing Outgoers were in relatively poor health but socially active as opposed to Frail Recluses, who were also in poor health but socially isolated.

The intent of gerontographics was to both define and empower a consumer-oriented older population by using a life-stage model to help marketers better understand the heterogeneity of the aging experience. The approach used revolutionary thinking to bring needed attention to the older adult market, to understand older consumers, to make them more visible, and to help them feel more seen, while criticizing the ageism that had overtaken the marketing industry in previous decades. The simplistic, reductionist, and frankly patronizing language that was used to segment older consumers, however, merely repackaged and rebranded stereotypical ageist characterizations of older people rather than eliminating them.[23] The effort is not dissimilar to *Allure* featuring editorial content claiming an end to anti-ageism next to ageist advertisements — which, as we have already seen, leads to cognitive dissonance.

Try this simple test to determine if the terms employed by gerontographics provoke ageism. Are you comfortable labeling your parent or grandparent a Frail Recluse or an Ailing Outgoer? Insensitive labeling of older people has been used with good intention in countless industries and disciplines, including my own. A couple of years ago I noticed that a longevity economics report describing the relationships among health, daily living activities, and housing needs used a continuum to describe older people as being in go-go, go-slow, slow-go, slow-slow, and no-go phases. Go-go people had excellent health and few limitations, while no-goers had poor health and lots of limitations and lived in institutional care. After several deep breaths and exacerbated sighs, I tried to explain the insensitivity of this approach to colleagues. It's hard to imagine many people feeling good about calling a loved one a no-goer.

Concepts like gerontographics reinforced the growing divergence in products and services being developed and marketed to third agers versus fourth agers. Healthy and active third agers were targeted consumers of products to maintain vitality and extend youthfulness. On the other hand, products and services for those in the frail fourth age were based on security and surveillance. I have noticed three distinct marketing techniques: "Let's do things that make us feel young"; "Let's get help for the things that make us feel old"; and "Please be worried about keeping Mom/Dad/Grandma safe." The third agers/successful agers in the first group are encouraged to go on vacation, buy a new car, or join the latest exercise or health craze. The fourth agers are pitched hearing aids or a back brace covered by insurance and are encouraged to consult with their doctor about the latest prescription medications. The last category focuses on loved ones of older people, who are encouraged to find peace of mind by purchasing products like technology that monitors health and safety.

In his book *The Longevity Economy: Unlocking the World's Fastest-Growing, Most Misunderstood Market*, Joseph Coughlin uses

Abraham Maslow's famous hierarchy of needs to illustrate that this deficiency-based tactic of developing and targeting the physiological health and safety needs of older people ignores unharnessed business opportunities to satisfy higher-order needs related to self-actualization, developing meaning, purpose, and the overall pursuit of growth and happiness. Coughlin states:

> By prioritizing the job of the consumer, longevity-economy innovators should be able to break free of the old narrative and address (older) consumers' upper-level goals and aspirations, not just fundamental needs.[24]

Countless opportunities await entrepreneurs and innovators seeking to profit from products and services that older people actually want — not just what we assume they need. Elderhood as a positive frame of reference offers literally limitless opportunities for product development and marketing in a world still dominated by an ageist mind-set.

As an aside, I would like to make a personal plea for someone with an entrepreneurial spirit to please (please, please) develop a birthday card line that celebrates, rather than denigrates, growing older. Birthday cards are among the worst offenders when it comes to ageist rhetoric with their misguided attempts at humor. *Isn't it funny that you are old, wearing a diaper, grumpy, and deaf? Happy birthday!* Changing the Narrative and the UK-based Centre for Policy on Ageing have launched anti-ageist birthday card campaigns. There are golden opportunities here, and I sincerely hope someone jumps on them. (P.S.: Party supplies could also use some attention.)

Seeing the invisible ageism within our larger culture and our daily gestures is the hard part. But once you see it, you can't unsee it, and once you are aware of it, you have conscious control over whether to give it power.

CHAPTER SIX

The (Mis)Information Age

Know that you are the perfect age. Each year is special and precious,
for you shall only live it once. Be comfortable with growing older.

— Louise Hay

My dad spent his thirty-year career as the head of the music department for a middle school in the New York suburbs of Long Island teaching kids who were in band and orchestra. In the 1990s, he was encouraged to incorporate technology into his classrooms and was among the first in his district to do so, although he lacked confidence in his ability to adapt. It took him about four months to get comfortable with the new equipment that allowed the students to experiment with special-effect sounds using a synthesizer. Also, as a composer, it took him several months to make the full transition from writing music and instrument parts by hand to mastering the software that helped him create and publish music. It was well worth it, though; he could now do in thirty minutes what had previously taken twelve hours. He hasn't looked back and has continued to learn with each new version and update of the music software that keeps him writing and publishing. Although he gets anxious at the sight of a notification that an update to the software is available, he takes a deep breath and presses forward.

The information age has added new layers to the ever-evolving story of aging and ageism. The digital age, with its concomitant advances in medical technology and pharmacological interventions, has provided unprecedented opportunities to enrich older people's lives. A new and growing field called gerontechnology has evolved, fusing gerontological practice and technology by embracing an interdisciplinary process of inclusive design to develop innovative products for older people. Tech ownership has grown rapidly among older people as smartphones, wearables, tablets, and smart speakers have proliferated, and health and wellness technology is helping people remain safely and comfortably in their own homes. Technology products like hearables (smart in-ear devices) have vastly improved quality of life for those who experience hearing challenges while simultaneously reducing the stigma and discomfort that come with wearing bulky hearing aids. Hearables provide an aspirational example of how a multipurpose tech product can appeal to all age groups; in addition to amplifying sound, they can be used for streaming music, monitoring fitness, and talking on the phone. Wearable technology has the potential to be an incredible tool to destigmatize disability through ubiquitous and multipurpose adoption.

Simultaneously, the sophisticated, fast-growing use of digital technology in its many guises has been determinative of social hierarchies that dictate societal norms and values. As a result, a new type of age discrimination in the form of digital ageism has evolved, adding new terms to our lexica such as *digital exclusion* and *technophobia*. Digital ageism represents prejudice from systemic biases that manifest through age-related exclusion in technology design and use.[1] Othering of age groups regarding digital media usage leads to generalizations and judgments and intergroup discrimination. For example, older people are seen by younger people as lagging in technological skills, interests, and capabilities, and younger people are seen by older people as inappropriately using technology with regard to content and time management.

Older people are widely perceived to be reluctant and resistant to adapting to the digital era. As with all other generalizations, this holds true for some older people and not for others. Regardless of personal affinity with the digital world, it is important to recognize that older people are not digital natives — a term that has been co-opted as an ageist code word perpetuating age discrimination — meaning that they did not grow up using computers in the classroom or at home. This fact alone does not make older people less capable of learning and adopting new technologies, but it can explain why there is a steeper learning curve. Research shows that the majority of older people feel technology makes a positive impact on society, but their lack of experience culminates in a scarcity of confidence in their ability to take up new gadgets and to navigate the online world.[2] This lack of confidence is widely perceived as ineptitude, widening the perceived digital divide and perpetuating stereotypes and prejudices based on age.

The Information Age and Digital Ageism

The Information Age, also referred to as the computer age and the digital age, is the period at the start of the twenty-first century that saw a rapid shift away from machine industrialization and toward digital technology. The Information Age began in earnest with the widespread use of the internet and personal computers in the 1990s, although development of the World Wide Web began in earnest in 1980. The ability to easily and rapidly share information resulted in a technological sea change with a swiftness and magnitude never before experienced. The prolific adoption of new technology has reached all aspects of human activity.

Digital divide is a term used to identify those who do and do not use the internet, and to what degree. The digital divide is not so much age-driven, as is widely believed, as it is a function of disparities rooted often in inequities and oppression. Internet usage has intersectional ramifications through demographic, socioeconomic, and health conditions: poverty, less education, poor health, and, yes, advanced age are all statuses associated with less usage.[3]

Attitudes toward technology are not the only drivers of adoption and usage; lack of access, underdevelopment of infrastructure, and limited broadband are structural factors that have a disproportionate impact on those who are poorer, older, and living in rural areas.[4]

Despite the fact that older people make up a significant share of technology users, lingering stereotypes and structural impediments reinforce the misperception that they are not interested in digital technology, disempowering them as a group and provoking further exclusionary stigmatization. As a result, an interesting and cyclical phenomenon persists in which older people are left out of the research and development process for applications that are designed for older people, which in turn suppresses use and leads to further stigmatization when older people fail to adopt products not because of disinterest but because they fail to address their wants and needs. Throughout history we have seen that well-intended but misguided attempts to *help* older people (without asking for their input) have contributed to ageist beliefs and behaviors. In the case of digital technology, the exclusion and disregard of older people decrease their desire and usage — the very opposite of what tech companies are setting out to accomplish. It is a bizarre merry-go-round.

Ageism in digital technology begins with the fact that younger people are the primary points of reference for identifying trends and practices. According to Statista, in 2016 employees' median age at top tech companies like Facebook, Apple, Amazon, and IBM ranged from twenty-seven to thirty-nine, not surprising given Silicon Valley's well-known youth-obsessed culture.[5] In 2007, Facebook's CEO, Mark Zuckerberg, said, "I want to stress the importance of being young and technical. Young people are just smarter."[6] Age-related discrimination claims in the tech industry are rampant and include accusations that tech giants exclude older job applicants by using age-restricted job ads and systematically laying off people over the age of forty. Shameful discriminatory practices and lack of age diversity inside the walls of tech companies plants ageism firmly within the culture. This structural and cultural ageism has vast consequences for the development and design of tech products.

Algorithms are developed by youth-dominated technicians. The human decisions driving the development of complex algorithms reproduce judgments and prejudices based on age stereotypes, which then become embedded within the digital system itself. As aptly stated by Cathy O'Neil in her TED Talk: "Algorithms are opinions embedded in code."[7] The fact that the vast majority of studies on digital practices don't include older adult voices or opinions exacerbates matters even further. As a result, big data, which is used to drive research questions and product development, may itself be ageist. Digital systems routinely monitor activity and generate information logs that in turn are used as input for artificial intelligence systems.[8] Just because there is a lot of data does not mean that it is representative of the behaviors and interests of the population as a whole. Big data is used to customize and improve digital products that rely on traits such as age, but as we have previously noted, when it comes to older people, we can't make any meaningful inferences in someone's behavior, preferences, attitudes, or usage based on their age alone. There is no such thing as a typical or average sixty-five-year-old or eighty-year-old who can serve as a model for generalization; there is simply too much variation and variability within the population. The problem is compounded by the common use of arbitrary age classifications (forty-five-plus, fifty-five-plus, sixty-five-plus) in research that homogenizes people into lumps. Yet again, we find another industry attempting to glean meaningful insights in consumer behavior by using broad age-based markers. If tech companies are not asking older adult consumers what works for them (in any kind of meaningful way), they are instead making guesses that are based on ageist assumptions. This is compounded further by the underrepresentation of diverse populations of older people whose members have intersectional identities based on gender and race. Lumping and categorizing in big data (and small data), excluding older people from working in the industry, and underrepresenting diversity among older people in the research and development process virtually ensures that ageism is interwoven into digital platforms.

Second-level digital divide refers to the discrepancy in information and communication technology competency between younger and older people. Inferring that older people are incompetent as a whole promotes ageism by endorsing ageist stereotypes and judgments. It also perpetuates self-directed ageism by provoking anxiety among older people questioning their capabilities. I will again refer back to the concept of stereotype threat and the phenomenon that we become the very stereotype that is thrust upon us. Communicating to older people that they are less likely to demonstrate competency becomes a self-fulfilling prophecy.

Around the turn of the new millennium, social media became ubiquitous. Social media platforms and applications enabled users to create and share content with friends, groups, or the public at large and have come to include social networking sites, forums, microblogging, wikis, and more. During the 2000s, social media use grew exponentially for all age groups as smart devices and mobile applications became more prevalent. Taking a page from the age-based market segmentation playbook, countless businesses claiming to be able to provide insights to drive generational marketing efforts appeared on the scene. With social media engagement a daily routine for most consumers, it makes logical sense for marketers to want to understand how generational preferences shape media habits. However, as we have learned, lumping people together based on manufactured and arbitrary generational classifications intensifies generational stereotypes and discord. Although age is one factor that shapes social media habits, they are affected far more by individual preferences and interests. Using age or generation to predict and classify behavior teaches people to give voice to stereotypes with regard to "other people," who are often deemed as fundamentally different or less than. The reality is that people over fifty now constitute one of the largest cohorts using technology to access social media. It has been reported that 76 percent of people aged fifty and older use at least one social media platform. According to Pew Research and AARP, among older adults, YouTube (73 percent) and Facebook (69 percent) are the most widely used platforms, followed by Instagram (37 percent), Pinterest (28 percent), and LinkedIn (27 percent).[9]

Despite the structural and attitudinal barriers inherent in the tech industry, the vast majority of older people (sixties, seventies, eighties, nineties, and beyond) are adapting to and mastering the internet, mobile devices, tablets, and smart technology. In particular, technology has been transformative for people seeking to stay connected with family and friends. Now that engaging with another human anywhere is but a click or voice command away, it is a cruel paradox that our virtual world, blossoming with opportunity for social contact, is often a very lonely place. Study after study shows that loneliness and isolation are an increasing problem that should be of great concern in our virtual world.

In an effort to capitalize on this trend, the nascent AI robotics industry has leaned into developing companionship products to substitute for human and animal connection. Robotic dogs, cats, and even seals are being marketed as interactive solutions to bring comfort and companionship to older people. Not surprisingly, these AI robotic products are promoted as therapy for "seniors," "the elderly," and "dementia patients," labels that evoke weakness, frailty, sympathy, and separateness. For the sake of clarity, referring to someone as a "dementia patient" is demeaning and diminishes a person's identity to that of a perpetual patient. To say that someone is living with dementia is a far more accurate way to describe the actual individualistic experience. As a gerontologist, I find robotic AI companionship products profoundly frightening. Their development signifies to me that we have entered the realm of robotic babysitting for older people, further removing older people from opportunities for actual human and animal connection. No matter how lifelike a dog or cat or seal (?) may appear to be, it cannot adequately supplant the touch, the feel, and the experience of real connection with another sentient being. Let us remember that older people, like people of all ages, need more than just a placating representation of connection to thrive. The dismissive notion that an AI substitute is enough to satisfy an older person's needs and desires sets us on a dangerous path to further embedding ageism as normative and acceptable.

Ageism and Loneliness

Humans have a biological, universal need for contact with others. Without it, skin hunger, or touch starvation, ensues. Interaction through touch has a variety of beneficial outcomes, including the production of serotonin, dopamine, and oxytocin, a neurotransmitter affectionately known as the love hormone. The need for touch is evident in early life and it is well known that attachment, or lack thereof, between infants and caregivers is critical to developmental outcomes, and physical touch is a vital component of the attachment process. A solid and secure relationship with a close caregiver in early life forms the basis of healthy social and emotional relationships.[10] When we feel loved, secure, and confident from a young age, we carry that with us throughout the entirety of our lives. The importance of attachment does not diminish in adulthood or elderhood.

We are endowed through our DNA with tribal instincts to attach to others for safety, security, and social enrichment. Without such connections, we are vulnerable to emotional hunger, a biological and psychological need that an artificially intelligent pet companion robot is not equipped to satisfy. Using technology to keep older people company represents a fundamental disregard for personhood, creates another barrier to finding meaningful ways for older people to contribute to the world, and is the epitome of ageism.

Social isolation describes the feeling we get when we lack fulfillment in our relationships or sense that we don't belong. Loneliness is the unwelcome feeling of discomfort and stress that we experience as a consequence of social isolation. Loneliness should not be mistaken with solitude, which is a purposeful choice to be peacefully alone. People of all ages experience loneliness at different points in their lives. Transitional life events can make people especially vulnerable to becoming isolated. Think back to the times in your own life when you underwent a major life change, like graduating from high school or college, moving to a new location, changing jobs, losing someone significant, or leaving the workforce. Such transitions increase the risk of feeling isolated or lonely, especially during the crucial months in their immediate aftermath. Now imagine feeling that same heavy ache of aloneness for days, months, or years on end. Chronic isolation and loneliness are quite detrimental to our physical and mental health and contribute to depression, distress, high blood pressure, and heart disease, among other things.[11] Many factors contribute to loneliness among older adults, and our predominant decline-based understanding of aging leads us to expect loneliness as we get older. Neither loneliness nor depression should be a normalized part of being old. Structural, cultural, other-directed, and self-directed ageism contribute to social isolation and loneliness, and yet as a society we barely acknowledge this reality.

A hallmark of social isolation is a lack of belonging. The construction and acceptance of ageism interwoven in our policies, laws, attitudes, and behaviors literally ensure that older people are systematically excluded from where we work, where we live, and what we value. We cannot be surprised that older people experience isolation and loneliness when we have created ageist systems that reinforce it. Segregating people based on age and ability, retirement denoting withdrawal as a life stage, normalization of anti-aging rhetoric that profoundly influences cultural standards of beauty, success, masculinity, and femininity, the construction of old age as a time of decrepitude and old people as a monolithic group, bias within the policies that drive our health care systems and that are embedded in our training pedagogy, and an information age built without the input of older people are all drivers of isolation. Over and over again we have minimized the importance and contribution of older people. This has resulted in an almost predatory consumeristic and deterministic model of telling older people what they should want and what they should feel they need. We have a dominant ideology that older people should be recipients of care, services, and products without surveilling their preferences and responding accordingly. In other words, we proceed as if it's okay to make everyday choices large and small for older people.

The robotic pet provides a poignant example of how we systematically view elders as the consumers of care and services. By making older people unidirectional recipients of products and services, we miss something essential to the impoverishment of everyone else in society — that health and happiness are built on reciprocity. We all have a need to give to others. Giving back is at the root of purpose, meaning-making, mattering, and attachment. Volunteering, for example, is not just about altruism. When we volunteer we don't just give our time and help, we also receive by gaining personal satisfaction and a feeling of value that comes from being of service to others. A lack of understanding and acknowledgment of elderhood restricts opportunities for meaningful social participation, keeping us stuck in seeing elders as takers and as others. The colloquial term *greedy geezers* speaks volumes, communicating that older people take without giving back. Ageist prejudices and stereotypes leave no room for belonging, thereby paving a well-worn path to late-life loneliness.

Shame and fear are inconspicuous enablers of isolation, too. Shame results from a negative evaluation of oneself and acts as a demotivating factor in participation in life. Feelings of being old (as society has defined it) invoke ideas of incompetence and irrele-vance and provoke fear of a blank stare from others as we try to make a point that goes unacknowledged and ignored. Shame is a powerful driver of human behavior because it is an extraordinarily unpleasant emotion. We can't avoid being old; it is an identity that we can't separate from; it takes over, superseding all other aspects of self. To cope, we use self-deprecation to point out our flaws before others can. We say things in good-humored fun like, "Forgive me for being late, I didn't remember where we were meeting — I'm old after all!" The simple act of belittling, disparag-ing, or acknowledging a self-perceived flaw acts as a shield to guard against potential attacks from others. We can give in to the idea that middle age is somehow superior to old age, making efforts to blend in with the dominant in-group — looking and acting younger, for instance, which is what the anti-aging industry would prefer we do. Or we quietly withdraw and isolate ourselves from the insults and the injuries. This is an illusion of choice. Self-remanded isola-tion can still be lonely.

My colleagues and I noticed age-shaming language and self-deprecation innocuously embedded in our own discipline of geron-tology. We conducted a discourse analysis of the 2015 White House Conference on Aging, which was recorded, as a mechanism to infil-trate and expose the ageism within.[12] We heard many examples of self-referencing shame or projecting a loved one's sense of shame. Here are a few outtakes:

> "How old is your mom?"
> "Mom is sixty-two, you're going to get me killed."
> ". . . no one will know, no one will know."
> "I'm now going to get myself into serious trouble at home. My wife was one of the ten thousand people yes-terday who enjoyed a birthday . . . uhh . . . and got to age sixty-five [laughter and applause]. I can say that be-cause I am only sixty-four [laughter]."

> "My mother is actually turning sixty-five and will be on
> Medicare next year, she will probably not like the fact
> that I mentioned that on a broadcast that is going
> nationally . . ."

We blame our own aging, rather than ageism, for perceived defi-
ciencies. Sadly, others laugh in agreement at our "jokes," perpetuating the cycle. Relational ageism is a contagion that spreads the
fear and shame that underlie isolation. Please don't misunderstand
— there is a time, place, and reason for self-deprecating humor,
which can facilitate bonding in a *we are all in this together* kind of
way. But calling out our oldness as a defense against judgment is
not a healthy use of humor. It teaches others that oldness is indeed
a shame that can't be shaken off, a shame that we will all feel if we
live long enough.

Feeling immense and intense shame, especially shame based on
a longing for a youth that we can no longer have, makes loneliness
a self-fulfilling prophecy. We become hypervigilant about social
rejection, and the lack of open dialogue about the relationship
between ageism and loneliness means that we end up self-isolating
more, hiding our feelings, and avoiding others, all behaviors that
lead to more shame. To diminish the age-based shame that we
carry around like heavy luggage, we first need to acknowledge that
it is there and that it is socially determined. There is nothing shameful about being old, acting old, and looking old. Having age pride is
a critical step in the journey to later-life empowerment. In my
presentations on ageism, I do an exercise where I ask everyone in
the audience to stand up and on the count of three, loudly and
proudly state their age. I have had people moved to tears during
this exercise, telling the group afterward that it never dawned on
them that they could take back power by owning their age.

Where you live can also make you more vulnerable to being
socially isolated. The physical landscape of our cities and neighborhoods determines our ability to access services and amenities. Not
surprisingly, the built environment creates inequities that disen-

franchise groups of people, most notably those who are subjected to institutional and historical oppression, such as people of color, women, and those living in poverty. Take a quick walk through a neighborhood with lower-income housing and you will commonly find broken sidewalks, overgrown landscaping, and poor lighting. Now try navigating this with any type of physical limitation or a walker or a cane. It is not only challenging to get outside, take a walk, and get some fresh air — it is dangerous. Tripping hazards abound, and moving about at nighttime is like trying to navigate a dimly lit obstacle course. Adding to your list of inconveniences may be that the nearest bus stop is blocks away with no seating or shelter in which to wait. Barriers to social engagement are built into the surrounding environment brick by brick.

The age-friendly movement was initiated to address the physical and environmental issues creating barriers for older people. The intent of age-friendly communities is to recognize that people thrive in accessible environments built for inclusion. Although driven by great intentions, misguided and inappropriate language, yet again, perpetuates ageist othering and exclusion of older people. Singling out age as the classifier for a friendly environment marginalizes older people by distinguishing their needs as different from those of people of other ages. We would see this clearly if we attempted to use the term *friendly* to connote belonging to a racial or gender group, for example. If the term *women-friendly* gets your hackles up, so should *age-friendly*. An age-inclusive environment, rather than friendly, is one that is welcoming to all. For example, a sidewalk designed with enough width to accommodate a wheelchair or walker is also ideally suited for a stroller. Common advice to get out more often, join a club, make a friend, or exercise is of little use when confronting a built environment that one cannot navigate alone. A lack of broadband and internet access for those living in some neighborhoods and in rural areas prevents people from socially connecting through technology as well. Anti-ageist efforts must encompass policy reform to address the structural barriers that restrict access to meaningful participation in society.

citizen [he was] willing to take a chance on [his] survival in exchange for keeping the America that America loves for [his] children and grandchildren."[1] My dad was angry, hurt, and personally offended that his life could be widely perceived as disposable based on his age. In the following days, the media was full of commentary and debate around whether it was just and prudent for older people to sacrifice themselves for the sake of the economy. If elders were the most at risk, in addition to being noncontributors to economic productivity, didn't it stand to reason that they should be required to remove themselves from society at large willingly? There were so many inaccuracies (based on unfounded biases) within that question itself, I didn't know how to begin with a cogent response. I will say once again that age alone is not a good predictor of health status and that older people provide substantive economic contributions as both consumers and producers. Here are a few eye-opening statistics from the AARP's Longevity Economy Outlook report:[2]

- People aged fifty and older contribute $8.3 trillion to the US economy each year, 40 percent of the gross domestic product. This will climb to $28.2 trillion by 2050.
- In 2018, people aged fifty and older held or created 88.6 million jobs in the US. This is predicted to grow to 102.8 million jobs in 2050.
- Spending by people aged fifty and older amounted to $7.6 trillion in 2018, which accounted for 56 cents of every dollar spent.

It is time to retire the outdated ageist mentality that older people are a drag on the economy and that their growing numbers signal the coming of a destructive wave that will lead to economic ruin.

Also, in March 2020, a worn-out and tired conflict between generations reared its ugly head when the term *Boomer Remover* began to trend on social media platforms. The term referred to

COVID-19 itself in response to news stories about the higher mortality rate among those sixty and older — Baby Boomers — who had become infected with the virus. At the same time, the media featured stories of irresponsible college-aged students — touted as Millennials — crowding beaches and bars for spring break, about to spread the virus to all parts of the country when they returned to their schools and homes, mostly in colder climates. Interestingly, those spring breakers were part of Generation Z — most Millennials are in their thirties — demonstrating the power of generational labels.

During the pandemic, the repercussions of age and ability segregation became crystalline. In February 2020, the first COVID-19 outbreak in a US long-term residential care facility led to hundreds of positive cases and more than two dozen deaths of residents, staff, and visitors. As COVID-19 spread throughout the United States, long-term care communities were hit the hardest, compounded by the fact that a susceptible population, based on medical frailty, were housed together and that the people who cared for them lacked appropriate personal protective equipment, or PPE. As staff in hospitals across the country were being recognized and celebrated as front-line heroes and efforts were under way to secure their needed PPE, the role and plight of the long-term care workers — their sacrifice and bravery and their need to be protected — went relatively unnoticed. Also unnoticed was the way structural ageism compromises those who dedicate their careers to working in long-term care communities. Because we devalue older people, we also fail to acknowledge the contributions of those who look after them with a living wage and proper resources. Moreover, the direct-care workforce disproportionately comprises individuals who have endured the effects of intersectional oppression, trauma, and a lack of societal supports.

The COVID-19 global pandemic has shined a very bright light on ageism. The response to the pandemic represented the accumulation of centuries of devolving attitudes toward aging and older people. In fact, the rampant displays of ageism in response to COVID-19 are what inspired me to write this book — I wanted to answer my own questions about how we got here. And by "we," I mean the global *we*. The ageist response to COVID-19 was pan-cultural and could be witnessed in most countries and cultures. So much of our shared histories brought us to this moment in time: the development of the social construction of old age, retirement as a life stage, the bifurcation of the third and fourth ages, the biomedicalization of aging, the fixation on caregiver burden, the normalization of age and ability segregation, and the manufacturing of generational tension. All these factors have shaped our understanding of what it means to age and to be old. All these factors influenced our collective response to a global crisis. COVID-19 was a flashpoint that made visible our deeply camouflaged, ignored, and accepted age-based biases. Every dimension and manifestation of ageism was on full display.

COVID Ageism

As the pandemic took over our lives and our newsfeeds, "the elderly" were portrayed as a homogeneous group of people with a high risk for succumbing to the virus. As we have learned through our tour of history, the term *elderly* had reverent beginnings in ancient times and morphed over centuries to take on derogatory connotations of presumed frailty and vulnerability. The term *elderly* is now regarded as an inappropriate and dehumanizing catchall that minimizes the diversity and individuality inherent within the population of older people. It is a decline-centric generalization that reduces the value and contributions of older people. Studies show people prefer the term *older adult* or *older person* over *elderly*, *senior citizen*, or *senior*, which homogenize an entire population.

Misinformation and ageist assumptions suggested initially that only older people needed to worry about the risks of the virus, which became widely discussed as an "old person's disease." Statistics from the Centers for Disease Control showed that the risk of death from COVID-19 was indeed higher for those seventy-five and older; however, the majority of positive cases were among those eighteen through twenty-nine, and fifty through sixty-four.[3] Younger individuals suffered devastating effects from the virus and thousands died, but that was the story less told.

An *infodemic*, a term describing the perils of misinformation spread by the press, social media, and public announcements by officials, exacerbated ageist rhetoric, including discussions about the morality of rationing care for the old as if they were more expendable than other age groups.[4] It is not uncommon for discrimination to flourish during times of scarcity when "those other people" are perceived as a threat to deplete limited resources. Through posts, tweets, and memes on social media, the infodemic firestorm of age-based bullying and separateness blazed.

Precisely which news items are fed to people on social media platforms is a function of algorithms based on each user's preferences and attitudes. These algorithms amplify confirmation bias as they present material that supports an existing point of view rather than challenges it.[5] Ignoring, or not being exposed to, dissenting information forms polarization based on misinformation and skewed information. Ageism is perpetuated by a cyclical pattern in which discrimination is continually reinforced. An evaluation by Maria Renee Jimenez-Sotomayor and colleagues of a randomly selected sample of Twitter posts from March 12 to March 21, 2020, provides a glimpse into the troubling public discourse about COVID-19 and older people.[6] Of the tweets analyzed, almost one-quarter contained ageist or offensive content toward older adults, and #boomerremover was tweeted more than four thousand times. One Twitter user said, "Calling #covid19 the Boomer remover should not make me giggle, but it does . . ." An analysis by Xiaoling Xiang and colleagues of Twitter posts yielded similar results, noting that more than one in ten downplayed the virus and implied that the lives of older people were less valuable.[7] Reading just a few examples of the posts identified in their study is enough to shock and appall:

> Individual species don't survive. Ecosystems survive. An ecosystem where the elderly parasitizes the young cannot survive. So the ecosystem throws out a virus and makes the whole system more livable.
>
> No one is arguing that old people should die or be denied treatment, but we shouldn't trade millions of lives to try saving the very old and frail from a virus. It's like an elephant jumping off a cliff to avoid a mouse.
>
> Quarantine the elderly, not the ones working, and let the young live again.

The trending and antagonizing commentary on social media demonstrated how generalizations toward age groups provoked ongoing generational tension. Most of the negative messaging targeted older people — "Coffin Dodger," "Boomer Remover" — but younger generations were also on the receiving end at times. News outlets reported concerning stories of Millennials and Generation Z flouting ordinances and disregarding safety measures with accompanying images of packed bars and overflowing beaches. Social media posts finger-pointed at the lack of caring and concern demonstrated by entire generations of young people. COVID-19 became yet another mechanism to highlight generational differences rather than engender unity.

As with ageism, oversimplified stereotypes about generations fail to capture any relevant information about individual variation or diversity of experiences. Within my age-diverse classrooms, I have witnessed many instances of older students teaching younger ones how to use new apps or how to navigate a software program. During the COVID-19 pandemic, we did not need to look far or wide to find countless examples of younger people demonstrating extraordinary care and concern for others. Younger people went grocery shopping for neighbors, visited relatives through windows and plastic sheeting, and made cards or wrote letters to people isolated by lockdown, often strangers, to convey solidarity and support. Despite the good deeds from younger people during the COVID-19 pandemic, many older people felt blamed by younger people for social-distancing protocols that became widespread for all, while at the same time feeling a heightened sense of vulnerability to the disease and also the changing societal and economic landscape. Ageism was evident in the evolving debate on mask wearing, which became politicized in a divisive way around individual freedom rather than unifying around collective responsibility. I was taken aback when public discourse focused more on self-entitlement at the expense of others than on social conscientiousness.

In 2020, as the pandemic raged, a deeply divided America was navigating a presidential election. With nerves on edge, the climate around campaigning was volatile. As part of an effort to engage young voters, ACRONYM, a progressively oriented nonprofit organization, resurfaced a "Knock the Vote" public service advertisement it had originally launched in 2018. The one-minute video showed a series of old people telling "Dear Young People" not to bother voting because "everything is fine the way it is." "Climate change? That's a *you* problem," one of the older actors sarcastically said. The horrifically ageist PSA demonizing older people was shared through social media and praised by many as comically savage. This despicable approach to mobilizing young voters did succeed at marginalizing and stereotyping older people and further pitted generations against one another. I continue to have great difficulty understanding how anyone believes that promoting generational contempt is a winning progressively oriented strategy to secure votes. It is absolutely absurd to assume that all older people lean to the conservative right and all younger people to the liberal left. This manner of binary thinking pigeonholes people and reinforces age and generational bias. It also summarily dismisses the foundational contributions of thousands of (now) older people who supported progressive causes and demonstrations such as the Civil Rights Movement, the Women's Rights Movement, the first Pride march in 1970, and antiwar movements.

The confluence of political divisiveness and pandemic age shaming worsened the already burgeoning problem of social isolation as older people were singled out to quarantine away from the rest of the world. Medical professionals joined in the growing discussion about the need to segregate those who were older and more vulnerable as the ever-increasing physical and mental health ramifications of isolation for everyone, in all age groups, became more evident. A group of infectious disease epidemiologists and public health scientists joined forces to author and support a plan for "Focused Protection" from COVID-19, publishing the Great Barrington Declaration.[8] Signed on October 4, 2020, many months into the pandemic, the declaration proposed to balance the risk of infection by allowing people at minimal risk of death to go about their lives normally, taking the basic precautions such as mask wearing, while simultaneously adopting measures to protect the most vulnerable, which included older people, or "retired people" as the declaration referred to them, as a homogeneous group. Their plan for focused protection was undoubtedly a well-intentioned attempt to address a very complex situation. The Great Barrington Declaration provides an example of how positive ageism and ableism can nonetheless promote othering and separateness. For example, the declaration states the following:

> Retired people living at home should have groceries and other essentials delivered to their home. Those who are not vulnerable should immediately be allowed to resume life as normal. Young low-risk adults should work normally, rather than from home. Restaurants and other businesses should open. Arts, music, sport and other cultural activities should resume. People who are more at

risk may participate if they wish, while society as a whole
enjoys the protection conferred upon the vulnerable.

Again, while well intended, the measures suggested essentially a
hierarchical system of value and access based on age and medical
vulnerability. Not to mention the reference to "retired people" as a
monolithic group. The declaration also fails by omitting reference
to or strategy for addressing the disproportionate burden of
COVID-19 on people of color, people in multigenerational households, people living in poverty, people without personal transportation, et cetera. In a critical piece, *US News* characterized the declaration as "when arrogance leads to recklessness."[9] Yet thousands of
medical and public health scientists and medical practitioners
signed on in support. The overtones and undertones of ageism and
ableism erected more barricades for older people to be seen and
heard, pushing the risk of social isolation to new heights.

The voices of older people have been stifled for decades. Ageism
has obstructed the individual agency of older people to the point
that we believe others are within their right telling older people
what they can and cannot do. Our caring nature tips over into
infantilizing behaviors quashing individual choice and limiting
personal freedoms. This dynamic is illustrated by a concept called
surplus safety, which describes the desire to reduce risks at all costs,
even at the expense of potential benefits.[10] Surplus safety can be
well intentioned — "Don't get up. I will get that for you!" — but it
can also lead to more stringent restrictions that impede opportunities for personal growth. Determining that it would be too risky for
an older person to work in their garden since they could possibly
trip or fall is a basic example. This overly controlling protective
behavior closes off a chance to enjoy life. Such an approach infan-
tilizes older people as incapable of weighing risk versus reward,
which is ironic given that they are the people with the most life
experience. For the most part, older people act quite reasonably
and are adept at evaluating a situation's risks.

The fact that surplus safety usually has positive, even loving motivations behind it provides another example of the depth and complexity of ageism. Positive ageism, also called benevolent ageism and positive age stereotypes, describes a tendency to label people of other ages in a positive but homogeneous way, such as wise, endearing, gentle, or adorable.[11] Positive ageism can also take the form of preferential treatment or access to benefits not afforded to other age groups, such as Medicare. Although such generalizations may seem kind or empathetic, they are simultaneously limiting and prejudicial. Positive stereotypes of older people commonly depict them as high in warmth, but such a view is also often paired with a perception of older people as being low in competence.[12] Positive ageism during the pandemic dictated behaviors aimed at protecting older people at the expense of individual agency and autonomy. Rather than look to older people to provide guidance and support based on their extensive life experience and advanced capacity for cooperative communication and skills-based coping, we instead resorted to marginalizing them further by taking additional steps to cordon them off as a group from the rest of society.

The dire consequences of social isolation were widely discussed during the COVID-19 pandemic, and a parallel pandemic of loneliness became a threat to individual and public health. No one was exempt from experiencing the stress, anxiety and emotional discomfort of social isolation. Lockdowns across the globe separated people from their families, friends, and neighbors. However, congregate living settings, like senior living communities and nursing homes, were hit particularly hard.

The virus's communicability meant that long-term care communities and hospitals needed to restrict visitors. Tragically, many older people became physically isolated in their rooms, apartments, and homes. Many died alone, from a variety of causes, without the comfort of their families by their side. The struggle to balance literal survival with all the things worth living for resonated throughout the public health emergency. To slow the virus's spread and "flatten the curve," social contact, social relevance, and social support came to a screeching halt for months on end. Swirling ageist discourse suggested that older people were the ones most vulnerable to isolation due to their lack of finesse with technology — sidestepping the underlying issues of inequality, intersectional oppression, limited access to social participation, lack of social capital, and the social determinants of health and of course, ageism that placed older people in a more precarious position in our culture to begin with.

Residents living in long-term care were not the only ones at risk of contracting the virus or that were feeling isolated. Staff working in congregate living environments faced multiple crisis points at work and at home. The story of ageism and COVID-19 must include a chapter on the degradation of those who provide support and care to older adults.

Devaluing People Who Care for Elders

Front-line caregivers, also known as health care aides (HCAs), have many titles, including licensed practical nurses (LPN), certified nursing assistants (CNA), and personal care aides (PCA). HCAs are the primary providers of care for older people in long-term care or receiving home-based support. HCAs account for a whopping 70 to 90 percent of staff in nursing homes and provide about 90 percent of direct care services.[13] Within long-term care settings, aides assist people who need help with walking, getting to and using the bathroom, bathing, grooming, and dressing. Aides provide the most intimate and personal care imaginable and play an integral role in maintaining the dignity and humanity of those for whom they care. Requirements for training and certification of aides vary by state; many states have absolutely no formally vetted training programs for some types of aides.

The diminishment of the importance of trained professionals

who provide care for older people can be made obvious by looking at rates of compensation. Physicians specializing in geriatric medicine earn less than half of some other medical specialists.[14] Nonetheless, these doctors sit atop the pay scale for geriatric professionals. The typical health care aide earns about $15 per hour, or below an estimated living wage of $16.54 per hour.[15] Almost 83 percent of care aides are female with an average age of forty-four. Many are single parents with limited childcare support, and many also provide care for parents or other family members. *Crunched for time, money, and physical and emotional resources* is an understated way to describe the life of many HCAs. To make matters more complicated, a growing number of care aides are hired on a part-time basis, eliminating their eligibility for health care benefits, sick leave, and paid time off.

Due to a lack of living wage, many aides live in poverty and/or need to work multiple jobs to survive. Adding another layer of difficulty, care aides are vulnerable to trauma due to their personal life stressors, work stressors, and life experiences. For example, care aides are more likely to be victims of structural and intersectional oppression as most are women, are people of color, and/or have received limited educational opportunities. On top of their own higher risk for personal traumatic experiences, they are at higher risk of experiencing secondary trauma that can result from working closely with others who have been traumatized.[16] Adding even more stress to their care roles is the daily exposure to frailty, vulnerability, illness, and death experienced by those for whom they are providing care.[17]

Care aides are the front line and the lifeline for many older and disabled people living in congregate settings or living alone, and they are systematically and institutionally devalued. The systems of care, as we have designed them, perpetuate structural ageism by de-prioritizing the needs of the direct care workforce along with the needs of older people, and COVID-19 exposed the cracks in an already structurally unsound care system.

As the virus began its relentless march to all corners of the world, hospital staff were appropriately hailed as the heroes of the day. In the early days of the pandemic, panic-filled news stories flooded the airways with pleas from hospital personnel begging for more PPE. Although the effort was slow to get going, people were listening and planning got under way to expedite the delivery of lifesaving protective gear to hospitals as quickly as possible. Simultaneously, long-term care communities were struggling with a wildfire of infections and a critical shortage of PPE. There was far less attention, action, or sympathy from public officials for the heroic HCAs and their predicament. Residents of congregate living communities and the people who cared for them struggled with the spread of infections. This in turn lead to critical staffing shortages. By January 2021, more than 136,000 COVID-19 deaths in the United States were among residents and staff members of nursing homes and other long-term care facilities.[18] That is 35 percent of all deaths up until that time. Thirty-five percent! There are certainly some obvious reasons for the high mortality rate in long-term care communities, such as the prevalence of underlying health issues and the susceptibility to spread with so many people living and being cared for in close proximity. But there are other, more insidious, reasons that are less acknowledged that stem from a lack of support for direct care staff, which in turn is an indirect result of ageism.

Since many direct care aides do not make enough money at one job to survive and since many are only hired on a part-time basis, often so employers and insurers can avoid having to pay benefits, it is common for aides to work multiple jobs at various locations. In a COVID-19 environment, multiple jobs spells disaster for transmission rates. If a staff member succumbs to illness, they are left in an often precarious position. Part-time jobs typically have little to no sick leave and little to no health insurance, which translates to the two painful options of either working while ill or going unpaid. Working while sick during a pandemic is unthinkable — but so is not feeding your family. Staff members, caught between a rock and a hard place, were often blamed and shamed irrespective of the difficult choices they made.

To make matters worse, even before the pandemic began most nursing homes did not meet the minimum staffing requirements suggested by the Centers for Medicaid and Medicare Services often due to staffing shortages.[19] For decades, it has been well documented that nursing homes receive minimal fines for violating regulations designed to protect residents; childcare centers commonly have licenses revoked for comparable violations.[20] With staff becoming sick and people needing even more individualized attention, staffing shortages increased and became even more problematic by affecting the quality of care and safety. Compounding the situation, training requirements for new direct care staff were minimized and condensed during the pandemic in order to remediate the critical shortage and meet the growing needs for caregivers. Simultaneously, aides were being condemned for contributing to the spread of the virus through poor infection control practices. The system was asking the impossible of the direct care workforce. Staff were shamed if they came to work sick, blamed if they didn't practice good infection control protocol, and required to pick up the slack in a dangerously understaffed environment. Ten months into the pandemic, nursing homes in every state continued to have a shortage of PPE with one in five reporting inadequate supplies when cases and deaths were at record highs.[21] Direct care staff are not to blame; administrators are not to blame; the system that supports structural ageism is. We have created a situation where those providing the most intimate, personal, and direct care to older people are overworked, underpaid, unsupported, and unrecognized. The complex nature of ageism has fashioned a world where an entire population of people is generally regarded as disposable, of little worth, inferior, and burdensome. By extension, the tendrils of disregard rooted in the system equally reach those dedicated to caring for its population. We have created a dangerous self-sustaining pattern of dysfunction that must be addressed.

The cycle begins with a systematic lack of extensive training requirements. Federal legislation requires at least seventy-five hours of training for CNAs and home health aides (an amount established in 1987 and unchanged since in twenty states), but there are no federally mandated requirements for training personal care aides.[22] States ultimately determine their own guidelines, and there is incredible variability in quality and rigor of state-sanctioned training programs and state certification exams. Much of the training time is spent in a physical or virtual classroom, with some hours devoted to clinical training in a practice setting but not many. Few programs incorporate demonstration of competence in caring for older people. Even fewer, if any, address the effect of attitudes about aging and biases toward older people in the training curriculum, and my research demonstrates why they should.

I surveyed about 750 people who work with older adults and asked them questions about their motivation for working with older people, how satisfied they were in their jobs, their education in gerontology, how likely they were to stay in their jobs, and how they felt about their own aging and older people. I found that training and education played an important role in why people choose to work with an older clientele.[23] Those with formal training were more likely to be motivated by feelings of personal reward and satisfaction, while those with little formal training were more likely to be motivated by the mere fact that a job was available — quite an important difference. Another enlightening finding had to do with the role that attitudes toward one's own aging and toward older people in general played in predicting job satisfaction and intention to remain on the job. In a nutshell, aides who *like* older people are more likely to be happy in their work and to stay on the job. Similarly, people who had less self-directed ageism and less fear of aging were more likely to be happy and to stay. Yet we don't inquire about attitudes in the recruitment process, nor do we provide meaningful training addressing these topic areas. Ageism at its very core factors directly into the chronic recruitment and retention problems in the elder care field.

Fighting ageism will require dismantling the whole ageist system of care as it is currently configured. The system could be vastly improved by hiring, training, valuing, and supporting the right employees in the right ways: First, ascertain attitudes about aging and desire to work with older people in the beginning of the recruitment process. Next, provide opportunities for training, reflection, and dialogue around how attitudes about aging influence happiness in employment. These are two simple, low-cost solutions that could have a meaningful impact. The potential cost-saving benefits of instituting anti-ageism strategies in recruitment and retention are remarkable. Hiring the wrong employee is an expensive proposition; the cost of a "bad hire" is calculated to be at least 30 percent of the individual's first-year earnings. Add the expense related to the time is takes to review applicants, interview, onboard, and train new employees and the total cost climbs steeply and quickly.

In the health care realm, the consequences of poor job satisfaction and high turnover are dire. When the quality of care is low, people suffer. Maintaining a dysfunctional system where nursing aides (and other types of staff) are overworked, stressed out, underpaid, devalued, and unsupported, as well as harboring negative attitudes about aging and older people, is doomed to failure. Ageism is responsible for poorer quality of care and lower quality of life for both those receiving and those providing care. Sadly, this systemic structural discrimination has a synergistic effect, with self-directed ageism resulting in more anxiety and negative health outcomes. Around and around the cycle continues.

An anti-ageist approach to improving the system of care can be found in a core and foundational gerontological concept called person-centered care. Person-centered care, also called person-directed care, is a philosophy that stresses the importance of centering the decision-making and goal-setting around the care recipient's needs and desires. It promotes a flexible approach to care that is built on relationship and reciprocity rather than the typical hierarchical system of provider-directed care. Person-centered care values individuality, autonomy, dignity, partnership, and privacy. It ensures that we meet the needs of each individual by asking personalized questions to establish successful systems of support. We know that using a person-centered approach promotes quality of life and life satisfaction. Ironically, although we often mandate that staff members take a person-centered approach to care with older clients, we fail to utilize that approach with support staff members. The principles of person-centered care can and should be used in training and supporting caregivers, and in the creation of anti-ageist environments. When staff members thrive, communities as a whole thrive.

CHAPTER EIGHT

Elderhood

The sooner growing older is stripped of reflexive dread,
the better equipped we are to benefit from the
countless ways in which it can enrich us.

— ASHTON APPLEWHITE

I t is my hope that I've helped you to recognize ageism in its many manifestations and to understand the very real threat it poses to our health and happiness. Now it's up to you. The creation of an anti-ageist world is within our grasp; each and every person who commits to investing time and thought and planning into their own aging and elderhood will add one more brick to the foundation of a solid and stable structure. We each can play an essential role in building the critical mass needed to effect change in policy, laws, and practice. You have already taken a critical first step: Recognizing ageism is the hardest part. When you see it, you now will have the awareness needed to change your relationship to it, to write your own story, and to create your own path to elderhood.

It is important for me to acknowledge that I am not an elder. I am a fifty-year-old gerontologist who is passionate about disrupting and dismantling ageism and ableism. I can't, and won't, begin to tell you what elderhood should look like or feel like for *you*. I honestly don't know what it will look like for me, but I can share the knowledge that I have gained from studying, investigating, and deeply reflecting on this topic. I know that there is no one path to elderhood and no one age in which a person becomes an elder.

Rather, elderhood is the culmination of our individual lived experiences and unique identities.

As described earlier, my mom had a jarring transition into a life of "retirement." However, her continued journey into elderhood has been marked with incredible growth and meaning. She shook off her disappointment in the lack of purpose retirement had to offer. She focused on reinventing herself by pursuing new hobbies, passions, and friendships. She now surrounds herself with friends who enrich her life, support her growth, and encourage her ambitions. Her path has led her to study new religions, write novels, and travel to new places.

Taking a personalized path to elderhood is a beautiful thing in that you get to decide what it means to you. Every one of us has been steeped in an ageist culture; the concept of elderhood is just now being explored and defined. There is much work to be done to fully grasp all of the developmental processes that guide us from adulthood to elderhood. There is much work to be done to normalize elderhood as a unique stage of life and an integral part of the life process.

Toward this end, I will share key insights that I have gained from years of reading, introspection, and meaningful conversations with people of all ages. I will also give you some ideas and approaches to help you shape your thinking about your own aging. Long-term solutions to ageism will require changes in laws, policies, and practices in government, health care, housing, business, marketing, technology, product development, and more. The type of monumental change needed does not happen overnight; it happens one person at a time until a critical mass of awareness is realized. Studying the movements that addressed race-based civil rights, women's rights, and LGBTQ rights reveals an ebb and flow of activity — two steps forward, one step back over a long period of time. Disrupting ageism will follow a similar trajectory and require similar persistence. Like other movements, defeating ageism is also about safeguarding your civil rights. The right to age with meaning and purpose, the right to be an active participant in society at all ages, the right to be heard and valued for your contributions at all ages. The anti-ageism movement requires you to think, feel, reflect, and practice again and again. Unlearning is far more difficult than learning, and it requires a willingness to become uncomfortable, even angry.

The journey from ageism to elderhood begins with first identifying your motivation. Take a moment to pause and take a deep breath and then ask yourself — *Why does this matter to me? Why do I feel compelled to climb aboard the movement to disrupt ageism?* To borrow from Simon Sinek's TED Talk and book, "start with why" to find your inspiration. For some of you the *why* will be personal. You want to maximize your own health, happiness, and well-being. You want to live that added seven and a half years on average of life afforded to those who possess more positive views of their own aging. Personal reasons can also extend to our care and love for others — you want those around you to enjoy the benefits of a rich and full life where every stage and age is celebrated and valued. Perhaps your *why* is motivated by social justice and equity and the desire for society to treat older people as equals. You might find that your *why* is driven from a business or economic perspective, recognizing that anti-ageism builds prosperity in workplaces and organizations. As you continue to reflect, grow, and age, your *why* will expand and deepen. My *why* as of late has morphed into an obstinate need to defy the effects of manipulation. I am working on self-care and being strong-willed as I age in a culture that tries to shame me and direct me as to what aging "should" look like. Whatever your *why* is, there is no wrong source of determination.

Gain Awareness

Once you have identified why it matters to you to recognize and fight back against ageism, you can then take the next steps to listen more closely to your thoughts and feelings. Begin by asking your-self these questions:

- How do you feel about yourself as an aging person?
- What do you think it means to be old?
- How do you talk about growing older?

You are not alone if your reflections on these questions elicit a vague sense of discomfort or unease. Difficult questions can trigger the stress response cycle, which is a biological reaction that happens when the brain perceives something that is threatening. We have been taught that aging is threatening when in truth, it is ageism that poses a danger. This stress response cycle induces the protective modes of fight, flight, or freeze states — anger, avoidance, or inaction. Because we have pathologized the process of aging, along with dying and caring, think about how your own aging has become a conditioned stimulus. Aging as a conditioned stimulus triggers a response of fear, shame, dread, and loss. It is no wonder it makes us uncomfortable and kick-starts the stress response cycle. Luckily, we can recognize the cycle and take steps to empower ourselves to disrupt it. In his book 7 *Habits of Highly Effective People*, Stephen Covey put it well: "Between stimulus and response there is a space. In that space is our power to choose our response. In our response lies our growth and our freedom." Using metacognition as a tool, we can learn how to tap into our own thoughts and become empowered to choose our response.

Metacognition simply means thinking about your thinking. Metacognition involves developing a critical awareness of what you think, how you think, how you learn, and how you make decisions. When we are exposed to stimuli, automatic processes kick into gear that override our conscious awareness and dictate our response. We are exposed to billions of stimuli every day, and our brains have the mammoth task of choosing what to focus on. Through the amygdala, the brain is designed to make inferences or categorize information very quickly — so quickly that our reactions may not be based on fully processed information or interpretations. Therefore, our first instincts typically include biases that we didn't consciously think about but that our brain unconsciously categorized. As our amygdala matures and stores memories and experiences, new information is efficiently sorted as either "safe" (things like me) or "unsafe" (things not like me). This innate brain function forms the basis of the implicit biases that invisibly drive our decision-making. Metacognition trains you to take a conscious step back, to take a deep breath, and to take the needed time to slow down your thoughts before they turn into judgments and behaviors. By gaining awareness of our thoughts and thought patterns, we can better control the desired outcomes.

Let's try a super-quick exercise to test out what I've just described. Think for a moment about how you feel about yourself as an aging person. Are you anxious about getting older? Are you hyper-focused on your perceived aging-related appearance? What feelings and emotions surface when you realize that you, along with the rest of us, are aging? Practice identifying the thoughts and feelings that arise, but whatever comes up, don't judge it, just be aware. Saying your thoughts out loud or writing them down in a journal can be enormously helpful in this process. Then start to question the origin of your feelings and thoughts. For example, if your gut reaction was fear or discomfort self-identifying as an older person, then go deeper to explore your assumptions. Where have you learned about aging and growing old? Did you have role models? Reflect on how those models for aging have influenced your thinking. To gain some perspective about aging, take a moment to think about how you have grown and matured over time. What have you overcome that you are proud of? How do you feel in your own skin today as compared with five, ten, or twenty years ago? Recognize that everything you have experienced that brought you to who you are today has been a part of your aging. With this acknowledgment, you can challenge your long-held assumptions that aging is only about loss. In just a few minutes, you can rearrange your thinking and rewire your brain. Once we have the ability and the skill needed to disrupt our patterns of ageist limitations, we can take the next step of looking to the future to focus on aging in the context of who we want to become.

Becoming

Once you have practiced slowing down your automatic thinking to gain awareness and insight into your own thought patterns, you can begin the next phase of designing your personalized aging experience. To get started, ask yourself this question: *What do I want my elderhood to look like?* I would place a wager that nobody has ever asked you this question before. Funnily enough, future-based questions are commonplace at other points in our life. We prepare our children for their future as adults. We ask children to dream about who they want to become, what they want to achieve, and where they want to live. Parents encourage their adolescents to envision their future and to manifest it by working hard, getting good grades, and staying on the straight-and-narrow path. We dream together as young adults about our careers, life partners, travel, and accomplishments. Somewhere along the way in midlife or beyond, we stop asking future-oriented questions of ourselves and others. Ageism and ableism keep us locked in and closed off to embodying our future possible selves in later life.

Possible selves is a concept that was developed by two scholars, Hazel Markus and Paula Nurius, as a mechanism to understand how the cognitive components of our hopes, fears, goals, and threats give meaning to who we would like to become.[1] Possible selves are intimately connected to who we were in the past and who we are today. The derivation of possible selves is bound by our individual sociocultural and historical experiences and influenced by models, images, and symbols in our immediate environment.

This means that what we envision for our future self will be inextricably linked to our individual life experiences and challenges. This is what makes aging, and elderhood, so special; it can, and will, look and feel different for each one of us. There is no template, or right or wrong way, to approach your vision of your future possible self in elderhood.

Structural and cultural ageism and ableism create a contextual environment that limits options for future possible selves in older age. The ageist and ableist world that we currently inhabit provides little hope of purpose, meaning, and contribution in old age. Our vision typically goes as far as a vague and fuzzy view of retirement as a final stage. We may plan for years to financially prepare for retirement; however, we less typically engage in emotional or psychological preparation. Given that average life expectancy is hovering at seventy-eight years of age, we could conceivably spend decades of our lives in older age. We are missing out on so many opportunities to carve our future paths.

The fear-based and shame-based culture of manipulation suggesting that aging is only about decline and loss is an encumbrance and barricade to the manifestation of future possible selves in elderhood. Ageism binds us to a visceral fear of loss and fear of relevance. Ableism obstructs acceptance of disability, dependency, physical decline, or deterioration. Our current understanding of older age is based on a decline-centric, withdrawal-based framework that promotes oppression of our future selves. Ageism and ableism have conditioned us to believe that aging is a slow and steady disengagement from society, relationships, productivity, and contribution.

As we have learned, aging is living, becoming, growing, and developing. In comparison, the process of dying is the cessation of living. Dying is a natural and normal part of life, as we are all mortal; however, the medicalization of the dying process keeps us from having conversations about our wishes, desires, and plans for a good death. We are afraid to talk about our inevitable destiny and

instead tie ourselves to a concrete anchor of denial. This is perpetuated further by the "F word" in relation to death — failure.
Remember that tabloid headline I mentioned about Betty White
"giving up on life" at ninety-eight? Death is not life's failure; death
is the final part of life's journey.

Vulnerability

It is a natural and normal part of the human condition to experience fear of death. Fear of death is a nuanced phenomenon
encapsulating various constructs like fear of the dying process,
fear of the unknown, and fear for those we will be leaving behind.
Fear of death represents the anxiety that we feel as a result of the
threats of nonexistence and the unknown — in other words, an
abstract fear. Although the fear of death is conceptually distinct
from the fear of aging, which includes anxiety over concrete
conditions like deterioration, dependency, and frailty, the two
fears are interwoven and the interaction between them contributes to other-directed and self-directed ageism.

To protect ourselves from the apprehension of death, we instinctively want to separate ourselves from the process of aging and those
who remind us of our vulnerable mortality. The coping mechanism
propelling us to seek shelter from the angst leads to a cycle of discrimination, first directed toward older people and then pointed at
ourselves. The other-based prejudice toward older people inevitably
takes an inward turn, resulting in the internalization of fear of death
and disassociation with aging, which is maladaptive and unproductive in the long term. We can try to hide from aging and death, but
we can't outrun them. Setting our intentions on accepting vulnerability, a good life during elderhood, and a good death is a far more
productive approach, however challenging this may be.

Interestingly, a healthy fear of death can inspire self-protective
behaviors that can be instrumental in prolonging life. Jamie Gold-

enberg and Jamie Arndt suggest a model of "Death for Health" that proposes the following: Conscious thought about death can promote health-oriented behaviors that ultimately decrease our focus on death-related thoughts and redirect thoughts and activity toward maintaining health, sense of meaning, and self-esteem.[2] Striking a balance between appropriate motivation from fear and destructive stress and self-injurious behaviors is critical. Cognitively separating the fear of death and dying from the fear of aging can help us embrace and prepare for both.

Embracing aging, rather than fearing it, turns the tables by providing us with endless opportunities for elderhood, living, growing, and becoming. The beauty of elderhood is that it allows for a fluid and dynamic way to view aging and older age because it provides for all versions of possible selves. Elderhood allows us full participation in meaning-making activities and relationships no matter our physical, cognitive, or socioeconomic statuses. It provides the space for us to understand and embrace that we can continue to become who we are with physical illness or cognitive challenges. Author Thomas Moore suggests that "illness is part of life, and feeling alive requires taking all that life has to offer, including sickness. It simply is. The illness is yours and it makes you who you are as much as your various achievements do. What can you do but receive the illness . . . as your opportunity to add one more piece to your character."[3] In an anti-ageist and -ableist world, we make space for people of all ages and abilities to thrive and make meaning *because* they have limitations, not despite their limitations. That alone is a subtle shift in thinking that could have a profound effect. Understanding aging as a multidimensional and multidirectional experience provides a starting point for accepting the inevitable changes we will undergo, both good and challenging.

Vulnerability, therefore, is not something that we need to treat or remedy but rather something that can be meaningfully embraced as a natural part of life's course. Vulnerability, physical, psychological, and spiritual, is an integral part of human existence.

Self-directed ageism and ableism result from the fear of loss and
vulnerability that we feel but don't acknowledge. It is so much
easier to brush the fear of vulnerability under the rug and avoid
negative emotion than it is to admit to ourselves that we are always
vulnerable. Instead, we do everything we can to look, feel, and act
young, able, and independent in an attempt to outrun inevitable
vulnerability.

Integration of Self

As we grow older, we experience dynamic change in four different
domains: biological, psychological, social, and spiritual. Understanding your aging as a holistic process with interconnected
spheres of human development helps to counter the dominant
narrative of aging as a singular process of decline. Viewing aging
as a biopsychosocial and spiritual phenomenon gives us the tools
to understand that aging is transactional. We are the culmination
of our experiences and influences in multiple and interacting
domains. Biologically our aging is influenced by our genetic inher-
itance and gene expression, our habits such as eating, sleeping,
and level of activity, and exposures to elements in our surround-
ings. Psychologically, the development of personality, mood states,
behaviors, and coping strategies influences the aging experience.
In the social realm, our environmental exposures, risk factors, and
protective factors are determinative. Spiritually, aging is affected
by how we conceive of ourselves and our sense of connection
with God, the Universe, or a higher power or consciousness. Each
of these areas overlaps, so that a change in one effects change in
the others.

The strengths-based concept of elderhood accounts for the
multidirectional states of change in all domains as we experience
later life. Using a biopsychosocial spiritual framework, it becomes
easy to recognize that it is impossible to define successful aging in

a predetermined way. There is simply too much nuance, variation, and diversification to warrant such a concept.

Whether we are successful depends in large part on how we individually define success. Successful aging is just as tenable for an individual living with dementia as it is for a lifelong marathon runner. There is joy to be found if you know where to look. I encourage you to take some time and think about your definition of success and what successful aging looks like for you. However, and this is gigantically important: As you think about what successful aging might mean to you, beware of common pitfalls and traps. The way that you define successful aging today, at your current age and stage in life, will reflect your present state of being rather than your future psyche. For example, let's say that you are an avid mountain hiker and your definition of successful aging is the continuation of the ability to hike. This makes good sense since the activity is important and meaningful for you right now. The thought of not having the capacity or ability to participate in challenging hikes might provoke anxiety or sadness; however, you are projecting that your future self will value this hobby and ability as much as your current self does. This may, or may not, be the case. As we grow older, we continue to enjoy some hobbies and activities and naturally transition away from others. Just because something is important to you now does not mean that it will hold that same level of importance later in life, nor does it mean that it will be integral to your personal experience of success. If you prematurely mourn the perceived loss of something and associate that loss with aging, you have fallen into the trap of projected distress. It is more realistic to recognize success as a fluid concept that you will define and redefine throughout your life. Envisioning success as an ever-evolving goal within the strengths-based framework of elderhood provides a healthy foundation that is both stable and flexible from which to view aging as a process of growth and resilience.

Resilience is the ability to adapt well in the face of adversity, stress, trauma, and change. There are many aspects of our lives and aging that we cannot control or modify. Focusing on resilience empowers us to get through difficult circumstances and to grow along the way. In some respects, we have a natural tendency to become more resilient as we age. As we grow older, we have a wealth of accumulated knowledge and experience to buffer us against the hard times. It is comforting to have the mind-set of "been there, done that, and I survived," or my personal favorite passed down from my parents: "This, too, shall pass." With age, resilience also grows alongside emotional regulation, and we have more dispositional resources. We can build a resilient mind-set throughout our lives by working toward keeping things in perspective, accepting change, reframing threats into opportunities, and increasing curiosity by removing judgment.

Being

Another way to prepare emotionally for elderhood consists of learning to focus on being rather than doing. We spend much of our lives in a hurried state of busyness — going, doing, accomplishing, checking tasks off the list, rinse and repeat. For those caught in the flurry of the never-ending cycle of doing, the transition to free time and an open calendar can be jarring. We are so busy doing for most of our lives that we forget to talk about, much less prepare for, a future state of being. As we grow older, we have an enhanced ability to choose what is most important to us and let go of activities and relationships that are toxic or unproductive. The positivity effect, described in chapter 2, allows us to see the positive aspects of life and the silver lining in situations more easily, providing a smoother path to finding happiness and contentment. There is also solid research and theory providing evidence that as we age, we develop the mental muscles to adapt to limitations while goal setting. The model of selective optimization with compensation, developed by Paul Baltes and Margaret Baltes, tells us that elders can successfully adapt to losses and grow through developmental opportunities.[4] Using the strategies of selection, optimization, and compensation, we learn to allocate limited resources in a productive manner that enriches our development. Through selection we decide which goals to undertake, considering any perceived challenges or losses that act as a barrier. We then optimize or refine our resources to achieve our goals. Finally, we compensate and find a new or alternative way to maintain functioning. For example, this can be as simple as a book lover with a visual limitation turning to audiobooks. It is unfortunate to realize that we can conceivably spend decades of our lives fearing losses, only to adjust to them with more ease than anticipated once they manifest.

Elderhood allows the space for people of different backgrounds, with different interests and different abilities, to be active participants in society. Doing so does not require us to be physically fit, independent, wealthy, or retired. We need merely to embrace who we are and make peace within ourselves by focusing on being and becoming. For some, becoming and being will mean engagement and activity; for others, meaning-making will consist of solitude and quiet reflection. The variation and individuation are endless.

Transcendence and Time

Swedish gerontologist Lars Tornstam described aging as a natural, developmental process that can lead to increased perspective, maturity, and wisdom. His theory of gerotranscendence (*gero*, "old"; and *transcendence*, "rising above") describes a developmental shift in perspective from one that is materialistic and rational to one that is more cosmic and transcendent.[5] This empirically based theory describes a developmental pattern encompassing shifting perspectives in three separate dimensions: the self, the relational, and the cosmic.

In the realm of the self, older age can bring opportunities to discover hidden aspects of the self and a new awareness of our positive and negative traits. Through self-reflection, individuals can experience a growing awareness of their own self-centeredness and recognize that we are a part of the universe rather than its center. Through the process, we can reach a fundamental acceptance of self, of life and the past, as a way to redefine reality. Often this process will allow us to focus less on the needs of self and turn to address the needs of others. This mirrors a concept introduced by developmental psychologist and psychoanalyst Erik Erikson called generativity, which poses that older people have a developmental imperative to nurture, give back to the world, and contribute to society and future generations.[6]

Regarding relationships, the need for superficiality fades away in later life and we are more particular about choosing to spend time in meaningful, authentic connections. Part of the gerotranscendent process can also include a desire for more contemplative solitude, which, as discussed earlier, should not be confused with loneliness or depression. Solitude can be a welcomed state providing the time and space for needed reflection for growth. During elderhood, we also experience a sense of freedom of self from societal limitations that previously kept us from speaking up or expressing ourselves. I have spoken with countless elders who have shared a delight in feeling the freedom to speak their minds, embrace their uniqueness, and carve their own paths. In elderhood, we shed the weighty self-imposed restraints that plague us in youth to fit in and conform.

As we age into elderhood, our cosmic understanding matures and provides opportunities for us to see and feel time differently, to connect to past and future generations, to be at peace with life and death, and to find joy in the mysteries of life and the mundane. The experience of time can change; we may revisit or reexperience earlier points in our lives. By doing so, we may be going through our own internal process of healing old wounds or reconciling past relationships. The subjective experience of time, how fast or slow time passes, can affect the quality and perception of our experiences.

Remember when you were a child and you were impatiently waiting for next week to arrive to celebrate something, or go on a trip or get your ice cream reward for good behavior? Next week was an eternity away. At seventy years of age, a week goes by in the blink of an eye. Time feels different because the subjective experience is different. At five years old, one week is a fourteen-times-greater amount of your whole life than when you are seventy. Put another way, at the age of five, one year represents 20 percent of your life. At the age of seventy, one year is just over 1 percent of your total life. This is one reason why we feel time so differently as we grow older.

I will sometimes say, "I feel so old," when I reflect on how my children have grown and feel a simultaneous sense of pride, awe, melancholy, and gratitude. I am trying to describe a complex mix of emotions that represent the saliency of time passing. "I feel so old" can describe what author Thomas Moore calls the first taste of aging, that first realization that your body, mind, or station in life has changed, that time has passed much more quickly than you realized.[7] This is in stark contrast with, and not to be confused with, the statement "I feel so old," describing feeling ill, tired, exhausted, or out of touch, which pathologizes and disregards the state of being old. A common question in gerontological research involves asking people how old they feel — a construct known as subjective age. My colleagues and I coauthored a paper describing this line of questioning as meaningless and unethical.[8] Asking the question "How old do you feel?" promotes ageism with a one-dimensional view of aging as decline. Feeling "old" can mean different things to different people. For example, feeling old just as accurately describes a sense of wisdom and knowledge as it does physical aches and pains.

On the contrary, old as a description of time passed contextualizes the experience of living and aging. Acknowledging elderhood as a state of development opens the door to accepting being old as a normal, and dare I say even desirable, state. We no longer need to disassociate with being old for fear of judgment but rather embrace old as a representation of time lived.

To add to the richness, complexity, and individuation of the aging experience, as we age, we are the culmination of all the ages we have ever been. This allows us to experience all of our ages at once. You will forever be the sixteen-year-old, the thirty-five-year-old, and the current version of you. This is a concept that my colleague Jenny Inker calls the convoy of selves and is described well by American writer Madeleine L'Engle:

> I am still every age that I have been. Because I was once a child, I am always a child. Because I was once a searching adolescent, given to moods and ecstasies, these are still part of me, and always will be . . . This does not mean that I ought to be trapped or enclosed in any of these ages . . . the delayed adolescent, the childish adult, but that they are in me to be drawn on; to forget is a form of suicide.[9]

The experiences you had at each age and stage of your life made you who you are today. Of course, we become less like each other and more like ourselves as we grow older; our idiosyncratic life stories ordain an unrepeatable path.

Roles and Contributions

One of the most troublesome hazards of using the construct of retirement to describe a life stage is that it leaves little room for the roles and contributions of elders. The tragedy is not only that this view impedes individuals from finding meaning but also that it prevents society from reaping the benefits of the lived experiences and knowledge of elders. There are, after all, a variety of human assets that increase with age, such as reflected experience, moral courage, patience, wisdom, emotional regulation, flexibility, plasticity, and big-picture perspective. Research has shown that as the brain ages in midlife and beyond, we begin to draw on more of its capacity for improved judgment and decision-making. In fact, the mature brain has several advantages over younger brains, including use of both of its sides more fully during decision-making, better impulse control, and emotional stability, in addition to the power of knowledge from decades of learning and life experience.

Acknowledging the gifts, talents, and potential of diverse elders, we can easily identify a variety of essential roles that require wisdom, counsel, economic, political, and interpersonal resources. In their writing and advocacy, geriatrician Bill Thomas and elder rights activist Maggie Kuhn discuss their ideas on roles for elders that provide an excellent backdrop to think about your *what* and *how*. Use the questions *what* do you want your elderhood to look like and *how* do you intend to find meaning and purpose as you think about your own future development as an elder.

In his book *Second Wind*, Thomas calls for a cultural revolution to redirect the dangers of the misconception of old age and radically reinvent elderhood. As part of his strategy, he suggests three critical roles that elders occupy, which can continue to be built upon in elderhood: peacemaker, wisdom giver, and legacy creator.[10]

As we age, we gain the ability to integrate our life experiences in a manner that broadens our views and allows us deeper perspective into multiple sides of an issue. As peacemakers, elders can capitalize on their integrative thinking to help promote peace and mediate conversation, helping people reconnect with each other and bringing context to complex situations. Peacemaking extends outward in our growing ability to help others and inward as we work toward the developmental imperative of making peace inside ourselves. Looking inward to find peace with our authentic selves, our contributions, and our gifts as well as our regrets and faults can be a meaningful process that prepares us for a good death.

The development of a legacy requires a journey of self-discovery that helps us determine how we would like to pass on our knowledge and wisdom. Legacy building occurs in the intimate space of inter-personal relationships and can also take place at the societal level through activism or stewardship. It often occurs as storytelling, as self-reflection, and through interaction with others. The quieter state of solitude described in the theory of gerotranscendence captures a state of being with the needed reflective space for an older adult to work through their life story, to make peace, and to acknowledge their legacy.

Giving time and sharing wisdom with those with less experi-ence is Thomas's third identified role for elders. Wisdom givers help others gain a sense of perspective. Aptly, wisdom giving is about having the ability and intuition to know when it is appropri-ate to share opinions, when it is judicious to simply reflect back on what was shared, and when it is most prudent just to listen.

In 1970, after being forced into retirement at the mandatory age of sixty-five, Maggie Kuhn formed the Gray Panthers movement to fight ageism and advocate for human rights and social and economic justice.[11] Kuhn was a transformative force who was motivated by her own experiences of oppression and galvanized by her enduring empathy and anger at the injustice perpetrated against those at the receiving end of discriminatory practices, especially elders. Kuhn believed that elders were particularly well suited to inhabit roles that focused on healing and humanizing society and that forged generational connections.[12] Volunteering is one role that we typi-cally identify as appropriate for elders, but Kuhn described many other opportunities less recognized and equally as essential. Described as the five M's — mentors, mediators, monitors, mobiliz-ers, and motivators — these roles are each brimming with inclusiv-ity and fluidity and can be perfectly designed for people of all levels of ability and interests; they can be tailored to issues of personal importance.[13] Not one requires of anyone to give more than they want to, and all offer limitless potential for purpose and meaning.

Mentoring is the role that we most often associate with elder-hood. It is easy to conjure up a mental image of an older person coaching youngsters in reading, tutoring them in math, helping to build a birdhouse, or teaching them to cook. This is a natural aspect of intergenerational relationships and enables us to share our lived experiences and accumulated wisdom. There are opportunities for us to stretch our expectations of mentorship to realms outside of relationships with younger people. Mentorship in business and entrepreneurship or workplace coaching with problem solving or relationship building could be invaluable.

The role of mediator provides an outlet for elders to help resolve conflict in political and personal spaces. If you have ever witnessed a calm grandparent stepping in to ease tensions during a heated situation between a parent and child, you can appreciate the compassionate understanding and affirmation that an elder can bring to a situation. With the benefits of aging come increased life experiences, exposure to multiple perspectives, and enhanced problem-solving skills, equipping elders to provide valuable perspectives in mediating conflicts in neighborhoods, schools, houses of worship, and organizations.

Monitoring provides ongoing scrutiny that preserves integrity and operations within institutions. Again, the benefits of experience gained during aging make monitoring an ideal role for many older people who want to engage socially and politically. Monitoring can include attending public meetings, reviewing legislation, and serving on nonprofit and corporate boards.

A mobilizer can thrive as an advocate for social change by helping to gather, organize, and assemble around meaningful causes.

Finally, elders as motivators can help move people from self-interests to a focus on public interest and collective well-being.

Society as a whole benefits from the knowledge and talents of elders. Regardless of the type of societal contribution, every day, all over the globe, in every local neighborhood, elders act as role models for what it means to age into elderhood and to grow old. Current elders can lead the way to an age-inclusive world by recognizing and sharing their gifts and talents and by simply allowing themselves to express their *oldness*. And the rest of us, who are striving to be elders in our own time, also have the responsibility to role-model what it means to age. One of the most effective and simplest anti-ageism strategies would be for each of us to take personal responsibility for embracing our aging and communicating our hopes, dreams, and wishes for our elderhood to others.

Because we live and learn in relational environments, our personal attitudes and behaviors have a profound effect on others. This impact extends to meaningful, close relationships as well as casual encounters in everyday situations. Although we are conditioned by the dominant cultural narrative, we individually have the ability, power, agency, and autonomy to choose how we respond and behave. With knowledge we have gained from practicing recognizing bias and from slowing down our thinking, and by using metacognition, we can take the next step to make small but meaningful changes in our behavior to be positive aging role models.

To become an effective role model, we first have to challenge our cognitive dissonance by recognizing when what we say and what we do don't match up. Cognitive dissonance occurs when we believe in two contradictory things at the same time. A few years ago, I read an article quoting a well-known actress discussing how Hollywood had a serious problem with ageism and limited roles for women over sixty. That same day, I also found an advertisement for an anti-aging moisturizer featuring the same actress with the quote, "Your anti-aging cream works fast? Mine works instantly!" Declaring ageism is a problem and promoting ageism all in one breath is cognitive dissonance. We all fall into this trap repeatedly. As role models for aging, we all have the responsibility to challenge our conflicting views and to work toward walking the walk and talking the talk.

A straightforward approach to role modeling is practicing saying what you actually mean rather than what is easily understood. For example, a common euphemism for describing a large number of older people in the population is *a silver tsunami*. Rather than using catastrophic language, it is just as easy to reference "the growing population of older people." The dreaded term *senior moment* is equally problematic; why not just say "I forgot" to express a temporary mental lapse? Give some thought to the idiomatic expression *young in spirit* and contemplate what young means versus what young implies. In this instance, we are using the word *young* to mean energetic, lively, engaged, or vibrant, so why don't we just say so? *Young* could just as well mean immature, labile, or inexperienced. This is certainly not a matter of political correctness; words have meaning and power that shape our understanding of the world and of ourselves. As a role model for aging, what we say carries weight. And to achieve the goal of an age-inclusive world, we must all share in the burden to do what is right and to acknowledge and challenge the cognitive dissonance that we hold. Being a role model for aging demonstrates to others that life, during every age and stage, has intrinsic meaning and extrinsic value.

Celebrate

It is hard to identify celebratory occasions delineating oldness as an achievement or milestone. At other ages and stages, congratulatory festivities acknowledge age-based accomplishments: the Jewish tradition of a bar or bat mitzvah at thirteen to celebrate the coming of adulthood, the Hispanic quinceañera at fifteen to celebrate the passage from girlhood to womanhood, and the Japanese custom of Seijin-no-Hi when twenty-year-olds are celebrated at a coming-of-age festival. Other celebratory rites of passage include graduation, getting married, having a child, and retirement. A rite of passage represents more than an occasion to have a big party; it is a ritual that marks a significant milestone, achievement, or change in life status. Ceremonies marking rites of passage provide a sense of belonging and can help people go through difficult transitions by providing support, encouragement, and a guidepost for expectations.

The celebration of milestones helps us gain a deeper awareness of life transitions and expectations while providing a sense of continuity with our own life story and a connection to the community. Rituals are integral components of rites of passage where participants enact a sequence of actions as a symbolic representation of being initiated, cleansed, or protected. There are several examples of rituals and rites of passage for elders throughout the world, but few are normative practices in Western culture.

Several Asian cultures have public rites and festivities that honor aging through late-life celebrations. In Korean culture a sixtieth birthday is directly related to the cycle of the lunar calendar and is celebrated as a day when you have completed the zodiacal cycle. The *hwan-gap* is the sixtieth birthday celebration in which parents are honored by their children. This is followed by *kohCui*, meaning "old and rare," to commemorate the seventieth birthday. Filial responsibilities are ritualized in Japanese and Thai culture with sentiments of love, reverence, and gratitude toward elders.[14] In Thai culture, *suebchata* celebrates longevity on the sixtieth birthday and every twelfth year following — seventy-second, eighty-fourth, and ninety-sixth birthdays. In Japan, the sixtieth birthday, *kanreki*, marks the completion of one life cycle and the beginning of the next. The eightieth year, *sanju*, and eighty-eighth birthday, *beiuj*, are also auspicious milestones.

Celebrations, rites of passage, and rituals can be important signifiers of longevity and elderhood. Recognizing milestones and markers throughout all of the stages of life instills a sense of meaning, value, and worth at all ages. In her book, *This Chair Rocks: A Manifesto Against Ageism*, Ashton Applewhite writes:

> It means acknowledging and embracing the actual process of change on which we embark the day we're born. Aging means living, and birthdays commemorate that happy fact.[15]

Western society does not need to culturally appropriate these specific customs but can be inspired by them to find unique ways of memorializing and celebrating the contributions of elders.

Time to Grow Up

Growing up, and out, of an ageist existence won't be easy. We will each face trials and obstacles as we unlearn the self-limiting ageist and ableist rationality we have been taught. By acknowledging and then embracing aging into elderhood as a process of continued evolution, we will learn anew and craft our unique persona and a personal vision for later life.

Individually we can start by recognizing the systemic nature of ageism in all of its forms and making the invisible visible. We can confront the fear, shame, and guilt that has shaped a culture with little understanding, appreciation, or motivation to grow past adulthood.

Ageism locks us into fear of our future selves and prevents us from living fully at all stages of life. Ageism poses limitations because it diminishes our sense of personhood and takes away our power, motivation, autonomy, and agency. Ableism keeps us rooted in unrealistic expectations that are impossible to achieve. We can learn, listen, reflect, and practice. And then we can be free.

We can begin to ask strength-based, growth-centric questions of ourselves and the older people in our life. Questions like: What are your goals? What gives you purpose and meaning? What will bring you joy today? If you want to change your worldview, change the questions that you ask of yourself and others. By asking these questions, we open the door to more possibilities than we thought could have existed in later life. We will spread the hope of mattering. We will listen attentively to those older than ourselves to soak in their wisdom and use that knowledge to keep growing into the people we hope to become. As we age, we will remember the child

within playing dress-up in big people's clothes and understand that
we will never stop developing as individuals, evolving into more
complex people — and that we should never stop striving to be
more authentic, truer to ourselves.

We can accomplish building an age-inclusive society by embracing the reality that aging equals change. Aging is knowledge. Aging
is confidence. Aging is perspective and freedom. We can reclaim
being old as the manifestation of a long life instead of a dreaded
state that we fear. We can welcome the natural beauty of our physically aging bodies instead of trying to erase the evidence. We can
allow aging to be a messy, imperfect, and unique experience. As we
age, we can acknowledge the vulnerability that leaves us feeling
exposed and scared of what comes next. I know it is not easy, but I
also know that it is possible. Where ageism is limiting, elderhood is
endless. Where ageism is claustrophobic, elderhood is the open air.
Where ageism is the disease, elderhood is an antidote.

Notes

Introduction

1. Tracey L. Gendron, Jennifer Inker, and Elizabeth Ayn Welleford, "A theory of relational ageism: A discourse analysis of the 2015 White House Conference on Aging," *The Gerontologist* 58, no. 2 (2018): 242–50.

2. Amy J. C. Cuddy, Susan T. Fiske, and Peter Glick, "Warmth and competence as universal dimensions of social perception: The stereotype content model and the BIAS map," *Advances in Experimental Social Psychology* 40 (2008): 61–149.

3. Becca R. Levy, and Mahzarin R. Banaji, "Implicit ageism," in T. D. Nelson, ed., *Ageism: Stereotyping and Prejudice Against Older Persons* (Cambridge, Mass.: MIT Press, 2002), 49–75.

4. Becca R. Levy, Martin D. Slade, Suzanne R. Kunkel, and Stanislav V. Kasl, "Longevity increased by positive self-perceptions of aging," *Journal of Personality and Social Psychology* 83, no. 2 (2002): 261.

5. Julie Ober Allen, "Ageism as a risk factor for chronic disease," *The Gerontologist* 56, no. 4 (2016): 610–14.

6. Becca R. Levy, Luigi Ferrucci, Alan B. Zonderman, Martin D. Slade, Juan Troncoso, and Susan M. Resnick, "A culture–brain link: Negative age stereotypes predict Alzheimer's disease biomarkers," *Psychology and Aging* 31, no. 1 (2016): 82.

7. Becca R. Levy, "Mind matters: Cognitive and physical effects of aging self-stereotypes," *The Journals of Gerontology Series B: Psychological Sciences and Social Sciences* 58, no. 4 (2003): P203–P211.

8. Susanne Wurm, and Yael Benyamini, "Optimism buffers the detrimental effect of negative self-perceptions of ageing on physical and mental health," *Psychology & Health* 29, no. 7 (2014): 832–48.

9. Geneviève Coudin and Theodore Alexopoulos, "'Help me! I'm old!': How negative aging stereotypes create dependency among older adults," *Aging & Mental Health* 14, no. 5 (2010): 516–23.

10. Becca Levy, "Stereotype embodiment: A psychosocial approach to aging," *Current Directions in Psychological Science* 18, no. 6 (2009): 332–36.

11. Catherine A. Sarkisian, Ron D. Hays, and Carol M. Mangione, "Do older adults expect to age successfully? The association between expectations regarding aging and beliefs regarding healthcare seeking among older adults," *Journal of the American Geriatrics Society* 50, no. 11 (2002): 1837–43.

12. Jennifer A. Bellingtier and Shevaun D. Neupert, "Negative aging attitudes predict greater reactivity to daily stressors in older adults," *The Journals of Gerontology Series B: Psychological Sciences and Social Sciences* 73, no. 7 (2018): 1155–59.

13. Joseph F. Coughlin, *The Longevity Economy: Unlocking the World's Fastest-Growing, Most Misunderstood Market* (PublicAffairs, 2017).

14. Coughlin, *Longevity Economy*.

15. https://www.havasgroup.com/.

16. Becca R. Levy, Martin D. Slade, E-Shien Chang, Sneha Kannoth, and Shi-Yi Wang, "Ageism amplifies cost and prevalence of health conditions," *The Gerontologist* 60, no. 1 (2020): 174–81.

17. Tracey Gendron, E. Ayn Welleford, Lynn Pelco, and Barbara J. Myers, "Who is likely to commit to a career with older adults?," *Gerontology & Geriatrics Education* 37, no. 2 (2016): 208–28.

18. Heather Boushey, *Unbound: How Inequality Constricts Our Economy and What We Can Do About It* (Cambridge, Mass.: Harvard University Press, 2019).

19. Adi Vitman, Esther Iecovich, and Nurit Alfasi, "Ageism and social integration of older adults in their neighborhoods in Israel," *The Gerontologist* 54, no. 2 (2014): 177–89.

20. Karin M. Ouchida and Mark S. Lachs, "Not for doctors only: Ageism in healthcare," *Generations* 39, no. 3 (2015): 46–57.

21. Stephanie E. Rogers, Angela D. Thrasher, Yinghui Miao, W. John Boscardin, and Alexander K. Smith, "Discrimination in healthcare settings is associated with disability in older adults: Health and retirement study, 2008–2012," *Journal of General Internal Medicine* 30, no. 10 (2015): 1413–20.

22. https://www.eeoc.gov/eeoc/history/adea50th/report.cfm?render forprint=1.

1. Complicated from the Beginning

1. Abdolrahim Asadollahi. "Quran on Aging," in Danan Gu and Matthew E. Dupre, eds., *Encyclopedia of Gerontology and Population Aging* (New York: Springer International, 2019), 125–29.

2. Sik Hung Ng, "Will Families Support Their Elders? Answers from Across Cultures," in T. D. Nelson, ed., *Ageism: Stereotyping and Prejudice Against Older persons* (MIT Press, 2002), 295–309.

3. David N. Keightley, *These Bones Shall Rise Again: Selected Writings on Early China* (Albany, N.Y.: SUNY Press, 2014).

4. https://www.sacred-texts.com/cfu/sbe03/sbe03181.htm.

5. Sarah Lamb, "Hinduism teachings and aging," in Danan Gu and Matthew E. Dupre, eds., *Encyclopedia of Gerontology and Population Aging* (New York: Springer International, 2019).

6. Jagriti Gangopadhyay and Tannistha Samanta. "'Family matters': Ageing and the intergenerational social contract in urban Ahmedabad, Gujarat," *Contributions to Indian Sociology* 51, no. 3 (2017): 338–60; Lars Tornstam, "Gerotranscendence: A Theoretical and Empirical Exploration," in L. E. Thomas and S. A. Eisenhandler, eds., *Aging and the Religious Dimension* (Westport, Conn.: Quorum Books, 1994), 203–25.

7. M. Hadas, ed. *The Basic Works of Cicero* (Modern Library, 1951).

8. Robert Hutchinson, *Poems of Anne Bradstreet* (Dover, 1969).

9. Mark E. Williams, *The Art and Science of Aging Well: A Physician's Guide to a Healthy Body, Mind, and Spirit* (Chapel Hill: University of North Carolina Press, 2016), 27.

10. Hesiod, *Theogony and Works and Days,* translated by Dorothea Wender (New York: Penguin Books, 1973).

11. Caleb Ellicott Finch, "Evolving views of ageing and longevity from Homer to Hippocrates: Emergence of natural factors, persistence of the supernatural," *Greece & Rome* 57, no. 2 (2010): 355–77.

12. Aristotle, *Rhetoric,* book 1, chapter 5. Summarized by anonymous in *British Medical Journal* 1, no. 4698 (1951): 135.

13. https://www.psychologytoday.com/us/blog/the-art-and-science-aging-well/201704/growing-old-in-ancient-greece-and-rome; Thomas R. Cole, *The Journey of Life: A Cultural History of Aging in America* (Cambridge, UK: Cambridge University Press, 1992).

14. Leslie Robert, "Anti-aging medicine: The history: The three avenues of gerontology: From basic research to clinical gerontology and anti-aging medicine. Another French paradox," *The Journals of Gerontology Series A: Biological Sciences and Medical Sciences* 59, no. 6 (2004): B540–B542.

15. Martin Lavallière, Martin, Lisa D'Ambrosio, Angelina Gennis, Arielle Burstein, Kathryn M. Godfrey, Hilde Waerstad, Rozanne M. Puleo, Andreas Lauenroth, and Joseph F. Coughlin, "Walking a mile in another's shoes: The impact of wearing an age suit," *Gerontology & Geriatrics Education* 38, no. 2 (2017): 171–87.

16. Laura L. Carstensen and Joseph A. Mikels, "At the intersection of emotion and cognition: Aging and the positivity effect," *Current Directions in Psychological Science* 14, no. 3 (2005): 117–21.

17. Julie Livingston, "Reconfiguring old age: Elderly women and concerns over care in southeastern Botswana," *Medical Anthropology* 22, no. 3 (2003): 205–31.

18. Livingston, "Reconfiguring old age."

19. Lazar Stankov, "Aging, attention, and intelligence," *Psychology and Aging* 3, no. 1 (1988): 5.

20. Carol Graham and Julia Ruiz Pozuelo, "Happiness, stress, and age: How the U curve varies across people and places," *Journal of Population Economics* 30, no. 1 (2017): 225–64.

2. The Era of Technology and Medicine

1. Kenneth J. Branco and John B. Williamson, "Stereotyping and the life cycle: Views of aging and the aged," *In the Eye of the Beholder: Contemporary Issues in Stereotyping* 4, no. 7 (1982): 364.

2. W. Andrew Achenbaum and Peter N. Stearns, "Old age and modernization," *The Gerontologist* 18, no 3 (1978): 307–12.

3. Glenda Laws, "'The land of old age': Society's changing attitudes toward urban built environments for elderly people," *Annals of the Association of American Geographers* 83, no. 4 (1993): 672–93.

4. Frank H. Nuessel Jr., "The language of ageism," *The Gerontologist* 22, no. 3 (1982): 273–76.

5. Melinda Hermanns and Beth Mastel-Smith, "Caregiving: A qualitative concept analysis," *Qualitative Report* 17 (2012): 75.

6. Susan M. Reverby, *Ordered to Care: The Dilemma of American Nursing, 1850–1945* (Cambridge, UK: Cambridge University Press, 1987).

7. Reverby, *Ordered to Care.*

8. https://www.ncoa.org/wp-content/uploads/8-3-12-US-of-Aging-Survey-Fact-Sheet-National-FINAL.pdf.

9. Frank Laczko, and Chris Phillipson. *Changing Work and Retirement: Social Policy and the Older Worker* (Open University Press, 1991); Warren S. Thompson and Pascal K. Whelpton, "A nation of elders in the making," *American Mercury* 19, no. 76 (April 1930): 385–97.

10. Cited in Achenbaum and Stearns, "Old age and modernization."
11. Keith Armstrong, "A history of the word 'handicap'" (London: Privately published, 2013). *Handicap* is a term deemed as offensive; it was first used in relation to people in the late 1800s to mean "defective."
12. https://www.history.com/topics/germany/eugenics.
13. Malcolm Johnson, "The social construction of old age as a problem," in Malcolm L. Johnson, ed., *The Cambridge Handbook of Age and Ageing* (Cambridge, UK: Cambridge University Press, 2005), 563–71.
14. https://www.cdc.gov/nchs/data/hus/2010/022.pdf.
15. Stefan Riedel, "Edward Jenner and the history of smallpox and vaccination," *Baylor University Medical Center Proceedings* 18, no. 1 (2005): 21–25.
16. Thomas P. Duffy, "The Flexner report — 100 years later," *The Yale Journal of Biology and Medicine* 84, no. 3 (2011): 275.
17. Carroll L. Estes and Elizabeth A. Binney, "The biomedicalization of aging: Dangers and dilemmas," *The Gerontologist* 29, no. 5 (1989): 587–96.
18. Estes and Binney, "The biomedicalization of aging."
19. E. V. Cowdry, *Problems of Aging: Biological and Medical Aspects* (Baltimore: Williams & Wilkins, 1939).
20. Johnson, "The social construction of old age as a problem," 566.
21. https://www.confrontingaging.com/1700s--1800s.html.
22. https://courses.lumenlearning.com/alamo-sociology/chapter/reading-the-process-of-aging/.
23. Marjory W. Warren, "Care of the chronic aged sick," *The Lancet* 247 (1946).
24. Ariadne A. Meiboom, Henk de Vries, Cees M. P. M. Hertogh, and Fedde Scheele, "Why medical students do not choose a career in geriatrics: A systematic review," *BMC Medical Education* 15, no. 1 (2015): 1–9.
25. Mary F. Wyman, Sharon Shiovitz-Ezra, and Jürgen Bengel, "Ageism in the health care system: Providers, patients, and systems," in Liat Ayalon and Clemens Tesch-Römer, eds., *Contemporary Perspectives on Ageism* (New York: Springer International, 2018), 193–212.
26. Robert N. Butler, "Psychiatry and the elderly: An overview," *The American Journal of Psychiatry* 132, no. 9 (1975): 894.
27 Jeff Greenberg, Tom Pyszczynski, and Sheldon Solomon, "The causes and consequences of a need for self-esteem: A terror management theory," in Roy F. Baumeister, ed., *Public Self and Private Self* (New York: Springer International, 1986), 189–212.

28. https://www.cmaj.ca/content/184/6/728; L. Diachun, L. Van Bussel, K. T. Hansen, A. Charise, and M. J. Rieder, "'But I see old people everywhere': Dispelling the myth that eldercare is learned in nongeriatric clerkships," *Academic Medicine* 85, no. 7 (2010): 1221–28.

29. Samuel Shem, *The House of God* (New York: Penguin Books, 2010).

30. Atul K. Madan, Shaghayegh Aliabadi-Wahle, and Derrick J. Beech, "Ageism in medical students' treatment recommendations: The example of breast-conserving procedures," *Academic Medicine* 76, no. 3 (2001): 282–84.

31. Becca Levy, "Stereotype embodiment: A psychosocial approach to aging," *Current Directions in Psychological Science* 18, no. 6 (2009): 332–36.

32. HR Rep. 109-337 (2005), https://www.congress.gov/congressional -report/109th-congress/house-report/337.

33. Atul Gawande, *Being Mortal: Medicine and What Matters in the End* (New York: Metropolitan Books, 2014), 6.

3. Entitlements: Ageism and Ableism at Work

1. https://www.merriam-webster.com/dictionary/retirement.

2. Robert C. Atchley, "Retirement as a social institution," *Annual Review of Sociology* 8, no. 1 (1982): 263–87.

3. Atchley, "Retirement as a social institution."

4. David Hackett Fischer, *Growing Old in America: The Bland-Lee Lectures Delivered at Clark University* (Oxford, UK: Oxford University Press, 1978).

5. https://www.newyorker.com/business/currency/the-real-reason -for-pensions.

6. Bayerisches Landesamt für Statistik, "Weiterer Anstieg der Lebenserwartung in Bayern" [Further increase of life expectancy in Bavaria], 2020.

7. https://www.ssa.gov/history/briefhistory3.html.

8. https://www.thebalance.com/the-history-of-the-pension-plan -2894374.

9. https://pensionresearchcouncil.wharton.upenn.edu/.

10. Dora Costa, *The Evolution of Retirement: An American Economic History, 1880–1990* (Chicago, Ill.: University of Chicago Press, 1998).

11. https://www.ssa.gov/history/age65.html.

12. W. Donahue, H. Orbach, and O. Pollack, "Retirement: The emerging social pattern," in C. Tibbitts, ed., *The Handbook of Social Gerontology* (Chicago, Ill.: University of Chicago Press, 1960), 350–51.

13. Oxford English Dictionary, https://www.oed.com/.

14. W. Andrew Achenbaum and Peter N. Stearns, "Old age and modernization," *The Gerontologist* 18, no. 3 (1978): 307–12.

15. Costa, *The Evolution of Retirement*; William Graebner, *A History of Retirement: The Meaning and Function of an American Institution, 1885–1978* (New Haven, Conn.: Yale University Press, 1980).

16. Graebner, *A History of Retirement*; https://profiles.nlm.nih.gov/spotlight/gf/feature/biographical-overview.

17. www.census.gov.

18. George L. Maddox and Elizabeth B. Douglass, "Aging and individual differences: A longitudinal analysis of social, psychological, and physiological indicators," *Journal of Gerontology* 29, no. 5 (1974): 555–63.

19. Atchley, "Retirement as a social institution."

20. Atchley, "Retirement as a social institution."

21. Costa, *The Evolution of Retirement*.

22. Elaine S. Fox, "Mandatory retirement — a vehicle for age discrimination," *Chicago-Kent Law Review* 51 (1974): 116.

23. Fox, "Mandatory retirement."

24. Jan C. Van Ours and Lenny Stoeldraijer, "Age, wage and productivity," IZA Discussion Paper 4765, 2010.

25. Rachael M. Klein, Stephan Dilchert, Deniz S. Ones, and Kelly D. Dages, "Cognitive predictors and age-based adverse impact among business executives," *Journal of Applied Psychology* 100, no. 5 (2015): 1497.

26. Claudia L. Satizabal, Alexa S. Beiser, Vincent Chouraki, Geneviève Chêne, Carole Dufouil, and Sudha Seshadri, "Incidence of dementia over three decades in the Framingham Heart Study," *New England Journal of Medicine* 374, no. 6 (2016): 523–32.

27. Anastasia Kononova, Pradnya Joshi, and Shelia Cotton, "Contrary to myth, older adults multitask with media and technologies, but studying their multitasking behaviors can be challenging," *Innovation in Aging* 3, no. 4 (2019): igz029; https://www.pewresearch.org/internet/2017/05/17/technology-use-among-seniors/.

28. https://crr.bc.edu/wp-content/uploads/2019/02/The-Business-Case-for-Older-Workers.pdf.

29. Becca Levy, "Stereotype embodiment: A psychosocial approach to aging," *Current Directions in Psychological Science* 18, no. 6 (2009): 332–36.

30. Thomas M. Hess, Corinne Auman, Stanley J. Colcombe, and Tamara A. Rahhal. "The impact of stereotype threat on age differences in memory performance," *The Journals of Gerontology Series B: Psychological Sciences and Social Sciences* 58, no. 1 (2003): P3–P11.

31. Robert Wohl, *The Generation of 1914* (Cambridge, Mass.: Harvard University Press, 1979), 203–9.

32. Karl Mannheim, "The problem of generations," in P. Kecskemeti, ed., *Essays on the Sociology of Knowledge* (Oxford, UK: Oxford University Press, 1952; original publication in 1928), 276–322.

33. Neil Howe and William Strauss *Generations: The History of America's Future, 1584 to 2069* (New York: HarperCollins, 1992).

34. https://www.nytimes.com/2019/11/27/business/millennials-care giving-retirement.html.

4. Retirement as a Life Stage and Successful Aging

1. Anna Vemer Andrzejewski, "'Selling sunshine': The Mackle Company's marketing campaign to build retirement and vacation communities in South Florida, 1945–1975," *Buildings & Landscapes: Journal of the Vernacular Architecture Forum* 27, no. 2 (2020): 59–82.

2. Claude Sitton, "Florida land fever becomes epidemic," *New York Times*, May 17, 1959.

3. US Census Bureau, Vintage 2018 Population Estimates.

4. Jane Freeman and Glenn Sanberg, *Jubilee: The 25th Anniversary of Sun City, Arizona* (Sun City, Ariz.: Sun City Historical Society, 1984).

5. Freeman and Sanberg, *Jubilee*.

6. http://media.corporate-ir.net/media_files/irol/14/147717/DelWebb/DelWebbBackgroundInfoFactSheet.pdf.

7. Elaine Cumming and William E. Henry, *Growing Old: The Process of Disengagement* (New York: Basic Books, 1961).

8. R. J. Havighurst, "Activity theory of aging," in R. H. Williams, C. Tibbits, and W. Donahue, eds., *Process of Aging 1* (New York: Routledge, 1963), 299–320.

9. Dan Buettner, *The Blue Zones: 9 Lessons for Living Longer from the People Who've Lived the Longest* (Washington, DC: National Geographic Books, 2012).

10. https://www.kff.org/medicare/issue-brief/how-many-seniors-live-in-poverty/; https://www.ncoa.org/article/get-the-facts-on-economic-security-for-seniors.

11. Robert K. Merton, "The Matthew effect in science: The reward and communication systems of science are considered," *Science* 159, no. 3810 (1968): 56–63.

12. Keren Brown Wilson, "Historical evolution of assisted living in the United States, 1979 to the present," *The Gerontologist* 47, suppl. 1 (2007): 8–22.

13. Brown Wilson, "Historical evolution of assisted living."

14. https://www.ahcancal.org/Assisted-Living/Facts-and-Figures/Pages/

default.aspx#:~:text=Number%20and%20Size%20of%20Communi
ties,in%20the%20United%20States%20today.

15. Jill Vitale-Aussem, *Disrupting the Status Quo of Senior Living: A Mindshift*,
Health Professions Press/AARP, 2019: 57.

16. John W. Rowe and Robert L. Kahn, "Human aging: Usual and
successful," *Science* 237, no. 4811 (July 1987): 143–49.

17. John W. Rowe and Robert L. Kahn, "Successful aging," *The Gerontologist* 37, no. 4 (1997): 433–40.

18. https://www.ncbi.nlm.nih.gov/books/NBK51841/#:~:text=Only%20
4.5%20percent%20(about%201.5,million)%20live%20in%20the%20
community.

19. https://medium.com/@entrepreneursway0007/101-inspiring
-quotes-by-zig-ziglar-448b8ab66865.

20. Lars Tornstam, "Gerotranscendence — a theoretical and empirical
exploration," in L. E. Thomas and S. A. Eisenhandler, eds., *Aging and
the Religious Dimension* (Westport, Conn.: Quorum Books, 1994),
203–25.

21. Peter Laslett, *A Fresh Map of Life: The Emergence of the Third Age*
(Cambridge, Mass., Harvard University Press, 1989).

22. Giuseppe Passarino, Francesco De Rango, and Alberto Montesanto,
"Human longevity: Genetics or lifestyle? It takes two to tango,"
Immunity & Ageing 13, no. 1 (2016): 1–6.

23. Organization for Economic Cooperation and Development, *Health at a
Glance 2015: OECD Indicators* (Paris: OECD Publishing, 2015).

24. Michael Geruso, "Black–white disparities in life expectancy: How
much can the standard SES variables explain?," *Demography* 49, no. 2
(2012): 553–74.

25. Gopal K. Singh, Gem P. Daus, Michelle Allender, Christine T. Ramey,
Elijah K. Martin, Chrisp Perry, Andrew A. De Los Reyes, and Ivy P.
Vedamuthu, "Social determinants of health in the United States:
Addressing major health inequality trends for the nation, 1935–2016,"
International Journal of MCH and AIDS 6, no. 2 (2017): 139.

26. Karen I. Fredriksen-Goldsen and Anna Muraco, "Aging and sexual
orientation: A 25-year review of the literature," *Research on Aging* 32,
no. 3 (2010): 372–413.

27. https://www.aarp.org/disrupt-aging/stories/ideas/info-2016/what-is
-old-video.html.

28. Jeff Greenberg, Tom Pyszczynski, and Sheldon Solomon, "The causes
and consequences of a need for self-esteem: A terror management
theory," in Roy F. Baumeister, ed., *Public Self and Private Self* (New York:
Springer International, 1986), 189–212.

5. The Era of Manipulation: Anti-Aging Culture

1. Herbert J. Rotfeld, "Fear appeals and persuasion: Assumptions and errors in advertising research," *Current Issues and Research in Advertising* 11, no. 1–2 (1988): 21–40.

2. https://www.globenewswire.com/news-release/2020/07/24/2067 180/0/en/Anti-Aging-Products-Industry-Projected-to-be-Worth-83-2 -Billion-by-2027-Key-Trends-Opportunities-and-Players.html.

3. B. Friedan, *The Fountain of Age* (New York: Simon & Schuster, 1993).

4. Todd D. Nelson, "Ageism: Prejudice against our feared future self," *Journal of Social Issues* 61, no. 2 (2005): 207–21.

5. https://thevisualcommunicationguy.com/2017/09/25/masculine -feminine-appeal-advertising/.

6. https://www.instyle.com/beauty/black-women-aging.

7. https://www.mentalfloss.com/article/67885/selling-shame-40 -outrageous-vintage-ads-any-woman-would-find-offensive.

8. Toni Calasanti and Neal King, "Firming the floppy penis: Age, class, and gender relations in the lives of old men," *Men and Masculinities* 8, no. 1 (2005): 3–23.

9. https://www.statista.com/statistics/264827/pfizers-world- wide-viagra-revenue-since-2003/#:~:text=Pfizer%3A%20Viagra%20 revenue%202003%2D2019&text=Pfizer's%20worldwide%20known %20erectile%20dysfunction,outside%20the%20U.S.%20in%202012.

10. https://www.gcimagazine.com/marketstrends/consumers/men/ FMI-Predicts-Extraordinary-Growth-in-Mens-Skin-Care-565440742. html.

11. Oscar Ribeiro, Constança Paúl, and Conceição Nogueira, "Real men, real husbands: Caregiving and masculinities in later life," *Journal of Aging Studies* 21, no. 4 (2007): 302–13.

12. Andrea Doucet, *Do Men Mother* (Ontario: University of Toronto Press, 2018).

13. Eugène Loos and Loredana Ivan, "Visual ageism in the media," in *Contemporary Perspectives on Ageism* (New York: Springer International, 2018), 163–76.

14. Loos and Ivan, "Visual ageism in the media."

15. Margie M. Donlon, Ori Ashman, and Becca R. Levy, "Re-vision of older television characters: A stereotype-awareness intervention," *Journal of Social Issues* 61, no. 2 (2005): 307–19.

16. Nancy Signorielli, "Aging on television: The picture in the nineties," *Generations* 25, no. 3 (2001): 34–38.

17. Denise D. Bielby and William T. Bielby, "Hollywood dreams, harsh

realities: Writing for film and television," *Contexts* 1, no. 4 (2002): 21–27.

18. https://stephenfollows.com/how-old-are-hollywood-screenwriters/#:~:text=Hollywood%20screenwriters%20are%20younger%20than%20directors%20(just)&text=The%20average%20age%20of%20the,35%20and%2045%20years%20old.

19. https://ppcprotect.com/how-many-ads-do-we-see-a-day/#:~:text=Fast%20forward%20to%202020%2C%20and,10%2C000%20ads%20every%20single%20day.

20. https://ppcprotect.com/how-many-ads-do-we-see-a-day/.

21. https://www.aarp.org/research/topics/economics/info-2019/longevity-economy-outlook.html.

22. George P. Moschis, *Gerontographics: Life-Stage Segmentation for Marketing Strategy Development* (Westport, Conn.: Quorum Books, 1996).

23. Stephen Katz, "Growing older without aging? Positive aging, anti-ageism, and anti-aging," *Generations* 25, no. 4 (2001): 27–32.

24. Joseph F. Coughlin, *The Longevity Economy: Unlocking the World's Fastest-Growing, Most Misunderstood Market,* PublicAffairs (2017): 136.

6. The (Mis)Information Age

1. Amanda Lenhart and John B. Horrigan, "Re-visualizing the digital divide as a digital spectrum," *IT & Society* 1, no. 5 (2003): 23–39.

2. Monica Anderson and Andrew Perrin, "Technology use among seniors," Pew Research Center for Internet & Technology (2017).

3. Amanda Hunsaker and Eszter Hargittai, "A review of internet use among older adults," *New Media & Society* 20, no. 10 (2018): 3937–54.

4. https://www.pewresearch.org/fact-tank/2019/05/31/digital-gap-between-rural-and-nonrural-america-persists/.

5. https://www.statista.com/statistics/653789/average-age-of-tech-company-employees/.

6. https://www.bostonglobe.com/business/2016/03/05/tech-job-market-hot-but-older-workers-struggle/775HPU2OYc5i0Jhr3TH-TqM/story.html.

7. https://www.ted.com/talks/cathy_o_neil_the_era_of_blind_faith_in_big_data_must_end?language=en.

8. Andrea Rosales and Mireia Fernández-Ardèvol, "Ageism in the era of digital platforms," *Convergence* 26, no. 5–6 (2020): 1074–87.

9. https://www.pewresearch.org/internet/fact-sheet/social-media/; https://www.aarp.org/content/dam/aarp/research/surveys_statistics/technology/2019/2020-tech-trends-survey.doi.10.26419-2Fres.00329.001.pdf.

10. Mary D. Salter Ainsworth, "The Bowlby-Ainsworth attachment theory," *Behavioral and Brain Sciences* 1, no. 3 (1978): 436–38.

11. Sharon Shiovitz-Ezra, Jonathan Shemesh, and Mary McDonnell, "Pathways from ageism to loneliness," in Liat Ayalon and Clemens Tesch-Römer, eds., *Contemporary Perspectives on Ageism* (New York: Springer International 2018), 131–47.

12. Tracey L. Gendron, Jennifer Inker, and Elizabeth Ayn Welleford, "A theory of relational ageism: A discourse analysis of the 2015 White House Conference on Aging," *The Gerontologist* 58, no. 2 (2018): 242–50.

7. The Era of a Global Pandemic

1. https://www.theguardian.com/world/2020/mar/24/older-people-would-rather-die-than-let-covid-19-lockdown-harm-us-economy-texas-official-dan-patrick.

2. https://longevityeconomy.aarp.org/?cmp=EMC-DSM-NLC-LC-HOM-FAM-20200129_LivableCommunities_899300_1269401-012920-F1-Longevity-CTA_Button-CTRL-4330516&encparam=L%2bZlhowiw4r5NBERDuVze8kLaFizIdheaqx117cOe3I%3d.

3. https://www.cdc.gov/coronavirus/2019-ncov/cases-updates/index.html.

4. Matteo Cinelli, Walter Quattrociocchi, Alessandro Galeazzi, Carlo Michele Valensise, Emanuele Brugnoli, Ana Lucia Schmidt, Paola Zola, Fabiana Zollo, and Antonio Scala, "The COVID-19 social media infodemic," *Scientific Reports* 10, no. 1 (2020): 1–10.

5. Cinelli et al., "The covid-19 social media infodemic."

6. Maria Renee Jimenez-Sotomayor, Carolina Gomez-Moreno, and Enrique Soto-Perez-de-Celis, "Coronavirus, ageism, and Twitter: An evaluation of tweets about older adults and COVID-19," *Journal of the American Geriatrics Society* 68, no. 8 (2020): 1661–65.

7. Xiaoling Xiang, Xuan Lu, Alex Halavanau, Jia Xue, Yihang Sun, Patrick Ho Lam Lai, and Zhenke Wu, "Modern senicide in the face of a pandemic: An examination of public discourse and sentiment about older adults and COVID-19 using machine learning," *The Journals of Gerontology: Series B: Psychological Sciences and Social Sciences* 76, no. 4 (2021): e190–e200.

8. https://gbdeclaration.org/.

9. https://www.usnews.com/news/healthiest-communities/articles/2020-11-06/when-scientists-arrogance-leads-to-recklessness-the-great-barrington-declaration.

10. William Thomas and Ronch, Judah, "Surplus safety," Lecture at The
    Erickson School, University of Maryland–Baltimore County master's
    degree course: The social and economic context of aging. August 2008.

11. Erdman Palmore, *Ageism: Negative and Positive* (New York: Springer
    International, 1999).

12. Amy J. C. Cuddy, Susan T. Fiske, and Peter Glick, "Warmth and
    competence as universal dimensions of social perception: The
    stereotype content model and the BIAS map," *Advances in Experimental
    Social Psychology* 40 (2008): 61–149.

13. Sarah L. Cooper, Heather L. Carleton, Stephanie A. Chamberlain,
    Greta G. Cummings, William Bambrick, and Carole A. Estabrooks,
    "Burnout in the nursing home health care aide: A systematic review,"
    Burnout Research 3, no. 3 (2016): 76–87.

14. https://www.nytimes.com/2016/01/26/health/where-are-the
    -geriatricians.html#:~:text=People%20avoid%20the%20field%20
    for,than%20half%20a%20cardiologist's%20income.

15. https://livingwage.mit.edu/articles/61-new-living-wage-data-for
    -now-available-on-the-tool.

16. Luis Manuel Blanco-Donoso, Jennifer Moreno-Jiménez, Alberto
    Amutio, Laura Gallego-Alberto, Bernardo Moreno-Jiménez, and Eva
    Garrosa, "Stressors, job resources, fear of contagion, and secondary
    traumatic stress among nursing home workers in face of the
    COVID-19: The case of Spain," *Journal of Applied Gerontology* 40, no. 3
    (2021): 244–56.

17. Michele M. Dreher, Ronda G. Hughes, Patricia A. Handley, and Abbas
    S. Tavakoli, "Improving retention among certified nursing assistants
    through compassion fatigue awareness and self-care skills education,"
    Journal of Holistic Nursing 37, no. 3 (2019): 296–308.

18. https://www.aarp.org/ppi/issues/caregiving/info-2020/nursing
    -home-covid-dashboard/.

19. Charlene Harrington, Mary Ellen Dellefield, Elizabeth Halifax, Mary
    Louise Fleming, and Debra Bakerjian, "Appropriate nurse staffing levels
    for US nursing homes," *Health Services Insights* 13 (2020):1-16.

20. https://www.washingtonpost.com/outlook/nursing-home-corona
    virus-discrimination-elderly-deaths/2020/05/07/751fc464-8fb7-11ea-9e
    23-6914ee410a5f_story.html.

21. https://www.aarp.org/ppi/issues/caregiving/info-2020/nursing
    -home-covid-dashboard/.

22. http://phinational.org/advocacy/nurse-aide-training-requirements
    -state-2016/; Sarah J. Hewko, Sarah L. Cooper, Hanhmi Huynh, Trish L.
    Spiwek, Heather L. Carleton, Shawna Reid, and Greta G. Cummings,

"Invisible no more: A scoping review of the health care aide workforce literature," *BMC Nursing* 14, no. 1 (2015): 1–17.

23. Tracey Gendron, E. Ayn Welleford, Lynn Pelco, and Barbara J. Myers, "Who is likely to commit to a career with older adults?," *Gerontology & Geriatrics Education* 37, no. 2 (2016): 208–28.

8. Elderhood

1. Hazel Markus and Paula Nurius, "Possible selves," *American Psychologist* 41, no. 9 (1986): 954–69.

2. Jamie L. Goldenberg and Jamie Arndt, "The implications of death for health: A terror management health model for behavioral health promotion," *Psychological Review* 115, no. 4 (2008): 1032.

3. Thomas Moore, *Ageless Soul: The Lifelong Journey Toward Meaning and Joy* (New York: St. Martin's Press, 2017), 274.

4. Margaret M. Baltes and Paul B. Baltes, "Psychological perspectives on successful aging: The model of selective optimization with compensation," in Paul. B. Baltes and Margaret M. Baltes, eds., *Successful Aging: Perspectives from the Behavioral Sciences* (Cambridge, UK: Cambridge University Press, 1990), 1–34.

5. Lars Tornstam, "Maturing into gerotranscendence," *Journal of Transpersonal Psychology* 43, no. 2 (2011).

6. Erik H. Erikson, *Childhood and Societ.* (New York: W. W. Norton, 1993).

7. Moore, *Ageless Soul.*

8. Tracey L. Gendron, Jennifer Inker, and Ayn Welleford, "'How old do you feel?': The difficulties and ethics of operationalizing subjective age," *The Gerontologist* 58, no. 4 (2018): 618–24.

9. https://www.goodreads.com/quotes/43474-i-am-still-every-age-that-i-have-been-because.

10. Bill Thomas, *Second Wind: Navigating the Passage to a Slower, Deeper, and More Connected Life* (New York: Simon & Schuster, 2015).

11. https://www.britannica.com/biography/Maggie-Kuhn.

12. Zalman Schachter-Shalomi and Ronald S. Miller, *From age-ing to sage-ing: A revolutionary approach to growing older* (New York: Grand Central Publishing, 2008).

13. https://biography.yourdictionary.com/maggie-kuhn.

14. Ronald Nakasone, "Journeying into elderhood: Reflections on growing old in Asian cultures," *Generations* 32, no. 2 (2008): 25–29.

15. Ashton Applewhite, *This Chair Rocks: A Manifesto Against Ageism* (New York: Celadon Books, 2019).

Acknowledgments

My journey to understanding ageism was enriched, guided, and supported by my incredible colleagues at Virginia Commonwealth University's Department of Gerontology. Thank you to Jenny Inker, Ayn Welleford, Jennifer Pryor, Faika Zanjani, Annie Rhodes, Catherine MacDonald, Gigi Amateau, Alexa Van Aartijk, and Jay White for years of meaningful, deep, reflective group thinking and exploration of this incredibly complex topic.

Thank you to Chip Fleischer and the Steerforth team for seeing the value of this book and for all of your ideas, help, editing, and support. I am grateful for the role each of you played in bringing *Ageism Unmasked* to fruition.

Laurie and Eileen, thank you for being by my side all these years as we have grown up together, learned from each other, and become the people we were meant to be both individually and within our own little collective.

Mom and Dad, you have been my biggest cheerleaders and my solid, unbending foundation for all of my years. You knew that I could accomplish what I put my mind to even when I didn't. To my brother, who will always be my Jeff of Honor, thank you for a lifetime of laughter, genuine caring, and for providing a space where I can always be goofy. To my children, Elijah and Rebecca, you amaze me with your warmth, humor, intelligence, passion for life, and ability to love. Watching you age and become yourselves continues to be the privilege and honor of my lifetime. To my husband, Chaz, my partner in everything, thank you for holding my hand and walking through the door to create the life we manifested. All my love as we grow old together.